Australian Dreaming Stories

ELLEN ANDERSON

As Recorded by C.W. Peck

ETT IMPRINT

Exile Bay

This edition published by ETT IMPRINT, Exile Bay 2023

First published in Australia in 1933 within *Australian Legends*
by C.W. Peck, Lothian, Melbourne
First electronic edition ETT Imprint 2023

Introduction copyright © Michael Organ2023
This book copyright © ETT Imprint 2023

ETT IMPRINT
PO Box R1906
Royal Exchange NSW 1225 Australia

ISBN 978-1-923024-46-5 (pbk)
ISBN 978-1-923024-47-2 (ebk)

Design by Tom Thompson

CONTENTS

Ellen Anderson with her husband Hugh, at Salt Pan Creek camp.

The Andersons (left) with other families at Salt Pan Creek,
Peakhurst, around 1925.

INTRODUCTION

"Don't think that the white man told us about God ... My people always knew about Him." (Ellen Anderson 1933)

These words from the octogenarian Aboriginal elder Ellen Anderson point to the lack of understanding and knowledge Europeans, and specifically the British, still had regarding the richness and complexity of Australian Indigenous culture, spiritual beliefs and story telling some 100 years after Captain Cook has sailed by and landed at Botany Bay back in April 1770. It would take another century for true recognition to come and for Indigenous story telling to be accepted as part of the nationls oral history and literary tradition. Prior to that, relatively small steps were taken, often by interested amateurs.

During 1933 *Australian Legends: Aboriginal Folk-Lore* was published in Sydney by a Thirroul school teacher, Charles William Peck. On the cover was a picture of two red waratah flowers, and inside twenty-five traditional Aboriginal Dreaming stories from southeastern Australia. Additional stories appeared in the *Sydney Mail* during 1931-2 and a second edition was published in 1933, bringing the total number of stories to fifty-two. This was a significant collection as they came mostly from areas around Sydney, which was the first region to be settled by Europeans in 1788 and subject to the most displacement of the Indigenous population and traumatic cultural decimation. Peck was no ethnologist, and the stories he presented were anglicised, the authors mostly unidentified, and there was scant reference to country or tribal and language affiliations. Peck only made specific reference to two Aboriginal informants. The first was Coomer gudgakala of Taralga, who is associated with one of the stories from the 1933 edition, and the second is Ellen Anderson, who is cited as informant for a significant collection of stories relating to the South Coast of New South Wales and published during 1932 and 1933.

Ellen Anderson was born at Unanderra, near Wollongong, on the coast south of Sydney, around 1846, the daughter of Biddy Giles and Paddy Burragalang. Her sister was Rosie Russell, later known as Queen Rosie of Illawarra, the wife of the last "King" of Illawarra, Mickey Johnson. Ellen grew up on the South Coast and later moved to the Georges River area, to Botany Bay and then to the mission at Maloga. Here she met her future husband Hugh Anderson, a Goulburn River man. They lived on the mission there, and later moved to Kangaroo Valley, near the Shoalhaven. During the 1910s Ellen and Hugh travelled back to the Georges River and purchased land at Peakhurst, near Salt Pan Creek. Ellen earned a living selling wildflowers, and this is likely to have brought her into contact with Peck, who was seeking to have the waratah proclaimed Australia's national flower. With the onset of the Depression in the late 20s and early 30s, the Andersons were forced to sell their land and set up camp in the nearby bush. Hugh died in July 1928 and Ellen at Salt Pan Aboriginal camp on 14 May 1931. She was aged 85.

In the prelude to the second edition of *Australian Legends,* Peck paints an affectionate picture of Ellen, referring to her as: "....the last full-blooded person of the Cammary Tribe .... she finds pleasure in the thoughts she has of her earliest childhood, and the knowledge she has of the real South Coast Aborigine. She is a princess, and she is also sister-in-law of the man who was the last king of the group... She knew many beautiful legends. But they had nearly all gone from her, for she never told them. She heard them and forgets nearly all. She hears no more, for they are seldom spoken of by the remnant of her race. Time was when the story-teller was an honoured man, when he dressed for his part, when the young people were educated in the lore of the land and the law of the land, by means of legend. But there is so much white blood in the people that practically none wish to hear the stories of the "Alcheringa", and so the stories have faded..."

Use of the word *Cammary* is likely an interpretation of

the Aboriginal Kamilaroi, the Indigenous name allocated to the region of northern New South Wales around the Namoi River. Here it is used in reference to the original tribes of Illawarra, which are more commonly referred to as the Dharawal / Tharawal or Wodi Wodi.

In her interview with Peck, Ellen notes: "...*My father came from the north and my mother from the south. His language was not the same as my mother's. I speak between the two. My words are both his and hers. Yours are neither. You speak like the people of far, far away. I do not understand you. But I know your words are of my country.*"

Ellen called her language Nungurra ilukka. The stories she told Peck and which are reproduced within this book, largely come from her childhood in the Illawarra and Shoalhaven, where she was raised in a largely traditional environment, though European settlers had occupied all the land around by this stage. They include the historical story (*At Low Tide*) of the first appearance of "white men" off the coast at Bellambi, where the *Endeavour* anchored on 28 April 1770 and Lieutenant James Cook and some of his crew attempted unsuccessfully to land; stories centred around native flora such as the waratah, Gymea Lilly and Danielle Berry; fauna including the kangaroo, koala, black swan, birds, a crayfish and a turtle; and the natural environment, such as in *What Makes Waves* and The First Bush Fire. In amongst these are references to travellers, local people and ceremony (viz., *Mulgani*).

The stories are often moral tales, providing guidance for the young people in regard to their place in Aboriginal society and the various stages of development they must go through. The majority are descriptive of the world around them, and obviously important in regard to survival. As such, a reading of the stories provides an intimate look into aspects of traditional Aboriginal life and custom. Beyond the mere story telling element.

As noted, the aim of the stories was to educate. Unfortunately, in stripping them of their cultural context, people such as Peck have diminished their value and accordingly presented the stories in terms of what is familiar to them, i.e., British folk lore, fairy tales, myths and legends. Of course, Australian Aboriginal Dreaming stories are anything but, being distinctively Australia, though with elements of storytelling that exist amongst traditional cultures around the world and that have been passed on to become part of contemporary story telling.

The impacts of colonisation had placed limitations on traditional Aboriginal story telling as a normal part of the education of children and young people. The resultant failure by Aboriginal elders to pass on stories was common in settled area, in part for fear of the young people being discriminated against because of their knowledge of, and practice in, traditional custom. Also, the white settlers placed restrictions on use of Aboriginal languages, custom and lore. By the time Peck came along in the 1920s to interview Ellen Anderson, his task was one of salvage during a period when it was widely held that the Australian Aborigines were a dying race. Despite the lack of cultural context of many of the stories, the fact remains that they are an important record of traditional story telling in an area of Australia where, unfortunately, much of that cultural heritage is lost.

Michael Organ
Murrumburrah
New South Wales
June 2023

References

Heather Goodall and Allison Cadzow, Ellen Anderson, The Dictionary of Sydney [webpage], available URL: https://dictionaryofsydney.org/entry/anderson_ellen.

-----, *Rivers and Resilience: Aboriginal People on Sydney's Georges River*, UNSW Press, Sydney, 2000.

[Obituary] Death of an Old Aborigine [Ellen Anderson], *Hurstville Propeller*, 15 May 1931; *Sydney Morning Herald,* 16 May 1931; *Illawarra Mercury*, 22 May 1931; *The Australian Evangel,* 2 August 1931.

Organ, Michael, *Illawarra and South Coast Aborigines, 1770-1990*, Australian Institute for Aboriginal and Torres Strait Islander Studies, Canberra, 1 December 1993, 348p.

-----, Australian Aboriginal Dreaming Stories: A Chronological Bibliography of Published Works 1789-1991, *Aboriginal History*, 18(2), December 1994, 123-44.

-----, C.W. Peck's Australian Legends: Aboriginal Dreaming stories of eastern Australia, *Australian Folklore,* 29, 2014, 53-69; ibid.,[blog], 23 June 2023, available

URL: https://michaelorganresearch.blogspot.com/2023/06/cw-peck-australian-legends-aboriginal.html.

Peck, C.W., *Australian Legends. Tales Handed Down from the Remotest Times by the Autocthonous Inhabitants of Our Land,* Stafford & Co., Sydney, 1925, 214p.

-----; ibid., second edition, Lothian, Melbourne, 1933, 234p. Digitised text available here: http://sacred-texts.com/aus/peck/index.htm.

PREFACE. A PRINCESS

In a little settlement for aborigines not far from Sydney lives the last full-blooded person of the once-powerful Cammary Tribe. She lives in the past. The present has no lure for her, and very little interest.

She has to eat and she has to sleep and she has to dress.

She looks for no pleasure, but she finds pleasure in the thoughts she has of her earliest childhood, and the knowledge she has of the real South Coast aborigine.

She is a princess, and she is also the sister-in-law of the man who was the last king of his group.

Both groups were of the one tribe, and each group had its king.

She has the true aboriginal cast of countenance, and she speaks most fluently to those who can understand or only partly understand the language of her people.

And her people are of two groups, for she said to the writer, "My mother was of the North; my father was of the South; I speak between the two."

And her English is of a pleasing kind, for it is not in any sense "pidgin." It is soft in accent and musical in tone.

She does not know her age, for, as she puts it, "I did not go to school."

She knew many beautiful legends.

But they have nearly all gone from her, for she never told them. She heard them and forgets nearly all. She hears no more, for they are seldom spoken of by the remnant of her race.

Time was when the story-teller was an honoured man, when he dressed for his part, when the young people were educated in the lore of the land and the law of the land, by means of legend.

But there is so much white blood in the people that practically none wish to bear the stories of the "Alcheringa," and so the stories have faded.

But not all.

And the religious beliefs?

They are still very real to this "Last of Her Tribe."

Just as real as ours are to us.

"Don't think that the white man told us about God," said Ellen.

"My people always knew about Him. Their fathers told them. Our God was never a wooden idol, nor a thing carved by human hands. He was always up in the Heavens where He lived, and from where He looked down upon all the world, and sought out the evil doers and punished them in many ways. From His throne He caused by His will the food to come upon the trees and the game to add to the larder. And He made the rain to fall, and He shook the earth with His thunder, and He threatened with the lightning. And there were good men who could see Him and get Him to move."

So said Ellen.

To pray to Him was the most natural thing for the people to do, and there were those whose principal mission it was to do that. They were the good men - the Clergymen, the Priests.

He made it the duty, too, of the people to inflict punishment upon the wrong doers that were caught and proved to be malefactors. Therefore it was, that men were sometimes stood up and speared, and women were beaten with nullahs.

There were the doctors, also. These men gave much time to the study and practice of the healing art, and sorcery and witchery did not escape their especial notice - just as the white people have their crystal readers and fortune-tellers to-day right in all our capital cities.

The doctors knew much of the effect of the eating of herbs and the drinking of water in which herbs had been steeped. They provided the leaves and the bark that were thrown into the water-holes in order to stupefy fish, as well as the medicines for the cure of the ills of the people. In their sorcery they played upon the emotions just as our mesmerists and evangelists do.

All this the old Princess of the aboriginal settlement tells, but not to everyone. Only to those who have a sympathy and an understanding, and a readable wish to learn the deeper things of the aboriginal mind.

There is, in a gully near Appin, a place that was sacred for, possibly, many thousands of years.

The gully is deep, and the head of it is a big round water-hole with precipitous sides, ever one of which the water pours in a roaring, tumbling, spraying fall.

The fall is governed now by the gates and spillways of the Cataract Dam, but until that was built it was governed only by the rains that fell and the winds that blew.

And the way down to the pool was always difficult.

None but the priest ever descended there, and when he did he carried with him the flint rod that served as the bell in the church steeple of the white man does - to call - but with the difference that the bell calls the people, and the flint called the gods or the spirits.

Tap, tap, tap, tap went the flint on the sandstone, and ages of tapping wore a hole that is not even seen by the great majority that clamber there now, much less understood.

My Black Princess heard of that Sacred Place when she was a tiny child.

She has never been to Appin, but her father and other great men of her group have been there and they told of the Sacred Spot when they returned to the coast.

It was a church, and nothing else, yet built, not with hands, but by the will of the God that the aborigines knew.

Our name for the Princess is Ellen, and Ellen's eyes glowed when she told the writer of her God.

And how they glowed when the writer told Ellen of the Sacred Spot near Appin, and when he showed that he knew the meaning of the worn hole and the ages of tapping.

"The place is 'kulkul,'" said Ellen, "and 'kurringaline,' and yet it is not 'pourangiling.' No 'kurru' are there."

A ROYAL VISIT

My office was very small, and very stuffy, though under the floor covering whenever I lifted it up, it was damp and mildewed.

The day was hot and steamy, and before me on the desk was a loose-leaf ledger that simply bristled and screamed with figures.

The headings were such as this: "30 x 5.77 Covers, 710 x 90 Covers, 30 x 31 B.E. Covers, many-figured Tubes," etc., etc., and the columns were serial numbers of tyres containing as many as nine figures. One figure denoted the year in which the tyres were manufactured, another the month, and intervening figures accounted for wealth of fabric or cord, and other details of tyre-building.

For we were distributors of motor-tyres.

The little half-door between me and the shop gave me a view of the counter; and the shelves, packed with little red bags, were heavy with their goods.

In the little red bags were the inner tubes.

Men came in and went out.

Some took price-lists. Some asked questions only, and then retired.

Some made a purchase and haggled about the discount, and some wanted to see the Chief.

My eyes ached and my head was not altogether free from a feeling like neuralgia.

The mildew, the heat, the figures-all were contributing factors.

Then I heard a voice that made me drop my pen and peer out towards that end of the counter near the door, and just out of my view as I remained seated and at ease.

As near to the outside door as she could stand while yet within the shop-that is the position taken up by the owner of the voice.

And such a voice! Smooth and soft and cushioned!

As velvet is soft to the touch, so this voice is soft to the ear. Perhaps not everyone's ear, but certainly to mine.

My twisting office-chair creaked as I stood up. Stood up to

attention as rigidly-hatless and coatless as I was - just as I sprang to it with a click when the General addressed me away over in Palestine.

"Nungurra ilukka," I said.

The owner of the voice-a lady-shy, timid, reserved, refined-turned to me.

"That is the language of my people," she said.

"Come here, please, and speak to me," I said.

Now I have heard some people snigger at the walk of those to whom this lady belonged.

It is certainly as different from that of most Sydney people, or any other white people, as the step of a peacock is from the tramp of a camel. It has the qualities of the peacock.

It is soft. It is noiseless. It is dainty.

It takes up its full share of the floor. Every toe finds its level, and the heel is planted as firmly as the supports of the Sydney Harbour Bridge.

As I said before, it is noiseless.

When I had found the lady a seat, and had resumed mine, I asked, "In what part of your country were you born?"

She answered evasively.

It is as natural for her and her people to be evasive as it is for the most shrewd of us to refrain from telling the whole truth when we want to sell a secondhand car or a groggy horse.

"My father," she said, "came from the South and my mother from the North. His language was not the same as my mother's. I speak between the two. My words are both his and hers. Yours are neither. You speak like the people of far, far away. I do not understand you. But I know your words are of my country."

Then she leaned forward and put a hand as soft as her footfall and as soft as her voice, on my shoulder.

She peered into my face and searched me as if she expected to see something she would be afraid of.

But she was not afraid.

"Excuse me putting my hand on your shoulder," she said. "Perhaps I have no right to do it. But I know now you do not mind, and you will understand."

Then her lips quivered and her eyes filled.

She leaned forward.

"You know my people?"

She questioned me.

Yet it was not really a question. It was a statement of fact.

"Yes," I said, "I know your people."

Then she overflowed.

"And aren't they GOOD people?"

It was an unburdening! It was a cry!

"Yes," I said. "They ARE good people!"

Then she removed her hat.

Her hair is white and old.

"My father was a King. I am a Princess. My blood is royal!"

"And where was your father a King?"

"He was a King of his people, and they lived around Wollongong. I am a native of the Wollongong district-born at Unanderra!"

"Was your father ever crowned?" I asked.

"Yes," she said, "when I was a grown girl-a young woman-he was crowned by the white people at a Wollongong Show. They gave him the title of 'King Mickey!'"

Then I saw a picture of my tiny boyhood.

In the Show ring, just after the high-jumping contest was decided, a black man was taken by the hand by a Wollongong dignitary and led to a small dais.

Some ceremony was enacted, but I was too small and too young to understand.

I saw that black man invested with something, and the people cheered and the black man shouted and waved his hands, and he had a string round his neck, and a brass crescent hung over his broad hairy chest.

"I saw your father crowned," I said, "and since then I have seen many of your people. They are GOOD people."

I bowed my royal visitor out.

She carried an inscribed copy of a little book about her folk.

"My grandchildren will read it to me," she said, "and I will come back one day, and I will tell you some more of our stories - stories we do not tell excepting to our own people. But I will tell them to you!"

"This," I said, "is a Royal visit."

She paused.

"Your people came here and took our country," she said very quietly, "but just a few of you understand us. I go now to Wollongong." My Royal visitor has been back to my office.

THE FIRST WARATAH

Why did the early arrivals in Australia imagine that the aborigines had no folk-lore, no legends, hardly any manners, habits and customs? Is it that they really had none, or that the blacks were merely incomprehensible? I think it was the latter.

Australia had much of country to be explored difficult country - on the Coast cool and equable of climate, on the highlands rough, jagged, and cold, on the Great Plains desert, with all the heat and madness of a great gravelled and sandy waste and the tales that may be told, known and unknown, are tales of endurance and adventure, rivalling truth and fiction of the sixteenth century.

One of the prettiest is the true story of Barrallier and its sequel. Barrallier carved his name on a gum-tree in one of the roughest of the foothills of the Great Dividing Range in 1802.

He was an officer in the Navy. He was fired with a desire to explore. But he was thwarted by his officers - the Commander refused him leave. Then did the Governor show that resource that is now supposed to be possessed solely by the Australian Digger.

The Digger, being British, but inherited it; and if the Tommy generally is without it, it is because Tommy generally is not Tommy specially.

Governor King learned of Barrellier's great desire, and as Governor King could make appointments irrespective of the naval commander, he gave Lieutenant Barrallier, R.N., the post of aide to himself. And then Governor Philip Gidley King, also R.N., sent his aide on an embassy to a mythical King of the Burragorang Tribe, away in those rocky fastnesses in the foothills of Australia's Great Dividing Range. Barrallier got down into that now far-famed Valley, and we, who do it in cars on a road blasted out of the side of a sheer precipice two thousand feet deep, wonder how?

There really was a king down there, and his name was Camoola. He was polite and eager to assist, if withal curious. He led Barrallier over a trackless defile, and showed the way up the rock walls by the track of the bush rat or the dingo.

But he developed a will to elbow Barrallier down into the ravine again.

No protestations availed to cause Camoola to continue in the direction Barrallier's compass pointed as the way to the interior. The white man grew angry; Camoola grew sullen. Camoola tried to tell something, even brandishing a spear, and Barrallier thought that demonstration a menace. Barrallier showed his teeth, and that night he was deserted. Sunrise showed that Camoola and his dusky satellites had vanished. The pointing of the spear was to illustrate that should the journey be continued another tribe's country would be trespassed upon, and war would be the result.

And Barrallier was in the thick gullied bush, surrounded by great forbidding walls of rock, and there grew the lovely *Prostanthera* (1) with it, purple baby-toothed flowers, the wild Clematis, the beautiful *Araucaria,* the laurel-like *Rapanea* (2) *variabilis*, the *Alsophila excelsa*, the myrtles, and that glorious plant and flower that to-day is the pride of every Australian who sees it and knows its history, and knows the fact that of all the world only Australia and Tasmania have it - have its whole genus - the WARATAH!

Its genus name was given to it by the great botanist Brown, and that was after it had been wrongly described as an Embothrium.

In 1818 Brown named the genus - which comprises three varieties - Telopea, because it is seen from afar; Queensland's waratah is *Telopewa speciosissima*; that variety also grows in South Wales, as also does Victoria's, which is called *Telopea oredes*, and the little beauty, the joy of the artist, is Tasmania's *Telopea truncata*.

But this little bit of botany is a digression.

Barrallier got out, and after reporting adversely of his black guides, he was returned to the navy, and his end came to him back in his native England, after being entrusted by the British Government with the task of erecting Cleopatra's Needle on the Thames Embankment.

Though he did not know it, we revere the name of Barrallier, and we glory in the deeds that were his. At the top of a rocky pass is his name cut in a giant gum-tree, and the date "1802."

Now for the sequel.

Many months afterwards a fine specimen of the Burragorang tribe found his way to a settler's house not far from Parramatta. He was none other than Camoola. And strange as it may seem, Camoola had had tidings brought him of Barrallier's adverse report. Two Hunter River blacks who were with Barrallier had returned to the Burragorang Valley with the story, and they taught to Camoola a little of the white man's tongue. He bore as a peace offering the national flower of his race - the only flower that the black man ever plucked to show a white man - the waratah.

And Camoola told its story.

Long years ago there lived a beautiful aboriginal maiden named Krubi. She had made for herself a cloak of the red skin of the rock wallaby, and she had ornamented it with the redder crests of the gang-gang cockatoo. It was said down in the Burragorang Valley to be the only cloak of its kind in the world. And Krubi knew of a man who was far enough removed in blood to be encouraged in his love for her. Her man had not yet been taught all that the corroboree was inaugurated to teach, but that did not prevent her from choosing a cleft between two great weathering sandstone rocks on the top of a ridge to watch for her man's return from the chase. The red figure was the first object to strike the eyes of the returning tribe of hunters. The red cloak was the only object looked for by the young man. But one night Krubi's heart was saddened. She learned that there was to be a great corroboree, and her man was to be taught what to do in war. Blacks from another tribe had been seen on Burragorang preserves.

They were to be punished.

Krubi of the red cloak stood on the sandstone cleft and watched for the return of the warriors. She heard the yells of battle. She saw here and there a flying figure, and sometimes she saw the swaying crowds down on the clear patches between the forest giants and tangled scrubs. Then in the afternoon she saw her scattered tribe of fighting men returning, and no young, lithe figure stepped out from the others and peered up as of yore.

Krubi stayed for seven days waiting, and her tears formed a little rivulet, and already the *Leptospermum* and the *Boronia serrulata*, and *Epacris longifolia* had begun to sprout. Krubi did not know their names, neither did Camoola, but Camoola showed the flowers - the Buttonflower, the Native Rose, and the Native Fuchsia and afterwards the botanists made the names.

Then Krubi went to the camp.

The ashes were cold and seven days old.

So Krubi returned to the sandstone ridge, and, with that power that the black man exercises, and that all mankind possesses, she willed herself to die. She passed into the little tract of weathered sandstone, and up came the most beautiful of Australian flora. The stalk is firm and straight, and without a blemish, just like the man Krubi died for. The leaves are serrated and have points just like his spear. And the flower is red, redder and more glowing than any other in Australia. The black man called it "waratah" because it is most beautiful. He loved it because he knew its history.

1. *Prostanthera*, the white variety of Tasmania is known as snow-flower.
2. *Rapanea variabilis*, a laurel, - *Alsophila*, a tree tern; *Araucaria cunninghami*, a pine tree; *Embothrium*, a family of red flowering plants in South America.

THE FIRST GYMEA
OR GIGANTIC LILY

One of the most wonderful of Australian flowers is the New South Wales variety of Gymea or Gigantic Lily (*Doryanthes excelsa*). This huge red bloom of ours is, as its variety name implies, the most gorgeous of the *Doryanthes genus* in this country.

The legend the natives have about it is as follows:-

One still, hot day in a summer of ages and ages ago, a tribe of aborigines found sustenance in a river-bed that lay at the bottom of a wooded ravine. The whole season had been droughty, and the water was hardly running at all. Yet there were holes, and great wide holes too, wherein the water was so deep that no one knew of any tree that would reach down to the bottom. Stones thrown in fell with a heavy, full-sounding splash and were sucked down and down. In those murky depths were huge eels and giant fish, and occasionally one or other came to the surface and fell a victim to the spears of the black men. The great towering, rock-girt side of the river gave many hours' shelter from the burning, blazing sun. That side with the easterly aspect was clothed with many myrtles and much *Macrozamia*[1] and *Chorizema*[2] and bracken fern. Quite a number of the dainty, feathery Christmas Bushes (*Ceratopetalum gummiferum*) shone gorgeous and red amid the *myrtaceae*, and rearing high above all the undergrowth were the giant eucalypti - the *Eucalyptus Smithii* with its long, narrow leaf, E. *Saligna* or Sydney Blue Gum, the Eucalyptus *australiana* or peppermint, and others - while wild clematis and Wonga wonga[3] vine climbed from shrub to shrub.

That day the heat was intense.

Nothing of the vegetation stirred, excepting during the silent wandering of a truant zephyr that came floating up the river-gully like the long, balanced, weightless gossamer that sways when the web is broken in the early morning.

The tribe lay about under the clematis and creeper and amongst the ferns. Only the hardiest of the hunting men stood, silent and perspiring, with poised spear, waiting for a fish to sail up to the top. Now and then a little chewed burley from the seed of the burrawang was softly dropped to the water.

Otherwise all was still.

Even the dogs lay stretched and asleep. They were too languid when awake to move with the shadows.

The fishing had been good. A number of splendid carp lay in a cool watered crack between the great flat rocks. When one of these fish appeared amongst the burley the thrust of spear was lightning-like. It made hardly a ripple, yet it pierced the water deep. It was so smartly withdrawn that the fish had scarcely time to cause even a bubble. By a dexterous heave it was landed, and it lay to kick its life away in that crack between the rocks.

Suddenly from away in the south-west a great billowing cloud hove into view above the cliff and above the gum-tops. Then the wandering zephyr became fierce. It swept on its way and brought down a shower of rustling leaves.

A haze, deep and sombre, crowded the scene. It was changed.

The fishermen glanced upwards, and then at one another.

They knew.

Up the gully came a boisterous gust. The placid water became a mass of dense ripples in a moment. They dashed their little wavelets in spiteful spray against the rocks. It was useless to fish any more. Besides, an eerie feeling was abroad. The dogs whimpered and huddled near some black or other-man, woman, or child., The old white-haired chief stalked out into the sand patch that lay athwart the dwindled stream, and cast a thoughtful glance at the heavens. The children cowered. The whole camp became astir, and yet no-one seemed to know just where to go nor just what to do. Women shivered and drew their 'possum rugs closer over their shoulders, and children's teeth chattered. They were susceptible and apprehensive.

Suddenly, too, the air was darkened, for the huge woolly mass of cloud had encompassed the whole firmament, and blotted out the sun. Gusts roared louder and louder. The myrtles seethed and rustled and quivered and bent before it. Huge tree-tops swayed and shook, and their interlaced branches tore and fought. A solitary bird high above essayed to cross the gully, but was swept from its course and whirled out of sight down stream. Now a great branch twirled and was snapped, and came crashing through the undergrowth and lobbed on the ground with a dull thud.

All the fishermen but one retreated. The one stood still. He was a mighty man and the son of a chief -

Then came the thunder. It pealed amongst the timber and amongst the people. With it came the blinding flash and the driven rain.

The chief led the way. The whole tribe rushed to a cave they knew of. It was formed by the rolling, some long years before, of three huge boulders against one another in such a way that an entrance was left, and inside was room for several hundred people. The last to enter was the chief's son. As he came another terrific crash of thunder and a fearful flash of lightning tore the world. Women put their hands to their eyes and ears, and children screamed. Men were struck dumb with terror. Peal on peal, flash on flash came, and then a deluge poured down outside, whilst the wanton gale swung the timber and felled the great gums. Then came the most awful flash of all.

In a lull in the downpour something happened. Flame and sound came at the same second. The clustering boulders were struck. A gum was splintered and shattered, and the whole earth, it seemed to the frightened tribe, was smitten, and it groaned and was hurled into space. The great masses of rock shifted, and the entrance was closed. Utter darkness fell in there. It was a thing that had never happened to their world before.

The chief's son now felt that he had to do something to prove that he was fit to rule when his old father passed away. The white-haired, wrinkled man was too spent with his years to do anything. Somewhere in the dark amongst his people he sat, and spoke not a word.

But the young man moved. He crawled cautiously inwards, his hands always scouting before him. If he touched a wall he turned and tried another direction.

He came to a passage so narrow and jagged that he cut his knees and his forehead. But he kept on. Once he had to pull away a stone or two in order to go further. At last he espied a thin streak of daylight. It came down from the top. It was very wispy, but up there somewhere was the light of day.

He listened.

There was no sound of thunder and no feel of rain. The giant storm had passed on down the gully more rapidly than it came. Outside a faint rumbling might then have been heard, but it was already far away. The appalling bursts of wind had passed on, too, and all was still again. Out of a clear, clean, blue sky the sun poured its westering beams across, and thick columns of swaying mists rose up into that space from which, as rain, they had come. Nature was smiling now, and the world was better for the storm. A mass of broken green and leafy twigs lay on the ground or were caught in the vines, and many floated, water-logged, on the pools. But down underground a whole tribe lay imprisoned and afraid to move.

All but the chief's son. He was now sensing the beauties of a clarified day outside because of the tiny streak of light that was with him. A little more pushing and he came to the bottom of a shaft. He could move a little debris and wrack, and he found that in the shaft he could stand upright. He could see the blue sky above. He stooped and coo-eed.

He was answered.

Then he lost his head, and he flung up his arms and commenced to climb. Like a rock wallaby he squeezed himself up and up. Pressing first one side and then the other, he forced his way towards the top. He loosened stones and rubbish, and they fell to the bottom. But he kept going on up. Near the entrance one boulder was poised. He placed his weight upon it and it was loosened. It crashed to the bottom, and that stopped any other person from following the chief's son. He nearly went down with it. A handy branch was his salvation. He grasped it, and with a mighty heave he was out of the pit.

He was saved.

And what of the rest? He leaned over and shouted. He heard the answer faint below. But the loosened sides were still falling. He tried all around and about, but there was no chance of getting between those enormous rocks. The marks of the lightning were upon them. A wonderful pattern of a tree was indelibly burnt into the stone, and is there till this day.

We have heard it said that the place is in George's River, somewhere behind Glenfield or Minto.

The sun sank as he does at the close of every day, and night fell quickly down in the river. Up on the boulders the chief's son slumbered.

Down below his people cried themselves to sleep. In the morning hunger took possession. Everyone must eat. The great fish still lay down near the water-holes. The escaped man sped there. He gathered up the fish, as many as he could carry, and took them up to the mouth of the shaft. Then he got some sarsaparilla vine, and with it and some rush he made a rope. Then he raced back, and began to climb the rock again.

He slipped.

Oh, agony! He was falling down, down. Crash! He rolled, and in rolling a jagged limb tore him badly.

He was pierced and his abdomen was cut badly.

But his thought for his people conquered the pain.

He got up again.

For days he fed them thus.

He grew weaker and weaker, but he fished and he fed the people. None could get out to him. He could simply lower as much food as possible. Some would live while others would die. This continued for many days. Those who told the tale to white men said that it lasted for a whole year.

Yet down in the prison the people were dying.

Then the tribe from Kurnell penetrated to behind Glenfield or Minto. They had found no opposition and no sign of the George's River blacks in any of their excursions for this whole year, so they became more and more emboldened, and the fishing and hunting were good. By the time they reached the place of the tragedy the chief's son was very ill indeed. His wound had never healed. He kept it open by his climbing up and his getting down. And the day came when the Kurnell blacks were very near.

He heard them.

He lay down under the shade of some Christmas Bush and Waratahs. The blooms were out and they shone red. He loved the waratah. He knew its story, and he had many times sucked the sweet nectar from its flowers. Beside him grew a little plant. He knew no use for it. But it was destined to be of great use to him.

Now up the stream he knew of a trickling spring. Another gully wound down its twisted way from above and opened into the bed of the river. It was very narrow, and in wet weather a little torrent splashed down from the flatter country above, and by means of a leaping waterfall it joined the more swollen river. Its sides were far more dense than the steep sides of the river. The *Leptospermum* flourished there, and waratahs were in crimson splendour. Out from a rock wall at the side gushed the spring. In dry times It simply was swallowed up in peaty ground beneath the tea-tree and *Leptospermum* and *Ceratopetalums*, but in rainy times it o'erbore them and joined the river.

A spirit often came out from that glen. It was speckled with glowing fires that flashed and were covered, and flashed and were covered, over and over again. The spirit was light and ethereal, for it could never be seen in its entirety and it could never be heard. All the tribe knew of it, and all held it in awe. All but the medicine man, and he, sometimes, when he had donned the mystic pipe-clay bands, went right up to the spring and talked with it there. When he came back he bore with him beautiful bunches of ferns of many kinds - *Hymenophyllum* and *Asplenium*, portions of the fronds of the *Dicksonia*, the *Adiantum*, the *Alsophila excelsa*, the Umbrella fern, the *Acrostichurn* and others.

It must have been the spirit that came to the hero of this legend, for as he lay exhausted someone took his hand and placed it on the little amaryllis that seemed to him to be of no use. Immediately it moved and grew. The leaves stretched up and up and became broader and broader. It was a wonderful happening. Many leaves came, each one long and broad and supple, and out from the central part came a long firm stalk. It grew up and up until at several feet a flower formed.

The young man's wound was more painful now than ever before. He pressed his hand to it and he found it to be bleeding. Then he swung his hand over to that wonderful plant again and it became red with his blood.

And it was warm.

It is always warm.

The young black slept. How long he slept no one knows. Whether it was for hours, or days, or years, has never been told, but when he awoke he was being well cared for. About his body was drawn one of the leaves of the *doryanthes excelsa*. Out from his mia-mia he saw many of these plants. They had come while he slept. All had leaves like bandages, and many had stalks with great red buds to crown them. They would be burst soon, and a flower as red as the waratah would be there.

Women came and peeped at him. Children saw that he was awake, and they laughed for joy.

Then a woman bent over him and deftly she wove another leaf bandage around him. The old fern-root poultices, dried up, lay around about. Then he knew who had tended him when he slept. And he felt strong enough to get up.

Close by were the fallen rocks. There was still no way in or out.

So the first Gymea or Gigantic Lily came into being, and not long ago men dug under the boulders and found a great heap of aboriginal bones.

1. *Macrozamia*-burrawang. 2. *Chorizema*-a yellow-flowered shrub.
3. Wonga-*Teooma australis*.

WHY THE TURTLE HAS NO TAIL

The Australian aborigines believed that the Milky Way was a "pukkan" or track, along which many spirits of departed blacks travelled to heaven, and that the dark place that we call Magellan's Cloud was a hole or split that occurred when the universe was frightfully shaken by some mighty upheaval which gave us many of the wonders of Nature, including the brilliant waratah, gorgeous caves such as Jenolan and others less magnificent, burnt patches of rock, and so on.

Legends also make mention of a hidden river, over which certain spirits have to travel to a Promised Land. This river flowed at the edge of a mighty forest, and beyond a fearful range of huge jagged mountains, at the nearer foot of which lay an extensive marshy lake, in the centre of which was an enchanted island. The natives of the South-East of Australia were very clear about the picture just described. They said that not only had some people spoken to returned men who had waded through the lake and been on the island and climbed the mountain and nearly reached the river, but they had also had amongst them at one time and another living men who had seen these fairy places and always knew that a continuous stream of spirits passed that way to the Unseen River.

Two giant trees grew on the bank, and a tortoise lay athwart it. Up to the time of this happening all tortoises and turtles had long tails. This tortoise reached from the bank just opposite the big trees, to the other.

On the journey many spirits were supposed to be in some way tempted to do evil, and succumbed to the temptation; therefore there were some fallings by the way. Some were kept floundering about in the lake itself, and these congregated on the island until they had expiated their sins, when they were allowed to go on. Others failed when climbing the mountain, and there on some barren peak they had to wait, while others remained faithful until reaching the lower level, and then were within sight of the river. But there was a test for them. They had to squeeze between the trunks of the giant trees, and then the bridge they reached was the tortoise.

Then came a time when many people quite good enough to get into heaven failed to reach the opposite bank of the river. It was known that they had got between the trees, and then all trace of them was lost; but one day a man arrived amongst the people who had been remade, and he told them his experiences.

He said that he had died and reached the tortoise on the unseen river. He stepped upon it, and was half way along it when it gave a sly jerk, and he fell off its tail into the river. He was borne along very swiftly, for it is a fast flowing stream, and suddenly he was swept underground. For a long time he was carried through deep subterranean passages, and at last he came out into sunlight. He found himself still in a river, and now it flowed between high banks, and playing in it were blacks that he knew. Some were just swimming, some were fishing, some were hiding in the rushes awaiting ducks. They did not know of his presence, though some seemed to hear him, for they suddenly became afraid and rushed off to their camp. At last he was swept into the sea, and a great wave washed him ashore. As soon as he touched land he found that he was changing. It took a long time, but at last he became a man again, and when he looked at his chest and felt his back he was aware of the scars that he 'had borne in his other existence.

He now suggested that when the next great man died - the chief or the doctor or the rainmaker or the clergyman - his best stone axe be buried with him.

Then a sorcerer came forward and proclaimed that he would undertake to go to the river and secure the passage of it for all time. He selected some other brave people, and by the aid of his sorcery he set out on the way of the spirits. He soon reached the forest, but found it full of the "little men of the bush." They barred the way of the party. Try as they would, no passage through the ranks of the "little men" could be made. So then they turned and followed the flow of the river, and that way no opposition was offered.

They came to a tree even higher than those at the crossing-place, and up that the great sorcerer climbed. From the top of it he could see the spirits stepping on to tail of the tortoise and some being shaken off. Many of these were taken by the claws of the hind feet of the beast and afterwards eaten. Others were carried down stream. The shadow of the tree was impenetrable to the "little men," and a bright star shed a beam to the tortoise.

The sorcerer saw that he must die before he could pass the little men and he and his party returned home. He sharpened again his axe. He put a sharpened bone in the fire, and scraped some of the burnt part off into his food. Then he died, and as a good spirit, he reached the giant trees, and there were no "little men" to stop him. But in their place was a great snake that reared its head and prepared to strike.

With a blow of his axe he severed the head from the body, and picking it up he squeezed between the trees and stepped on to the tail of the tortoise. When he was about half way over, just as he had seen it do to others, and just as the returned man had told it did to him, it gave a great shake. But he was wary, and with another great blow of his axe he cut the tail off. Quickly rushing to the other bank he turned and swung the axe at the head of the tortoise and that was severed too. Of this, though, he repented, and as the head swung down the stream he put the head of the snake in its place. Then the beast rolled over and sank out of sight.

And so now all tortoises and turtles have a snake's head and are tail-less.

And if the last woman of the Illawarra Group, who is still living, is asked about it, and if all the points of the story are examined, it will be found that there is as much truth as fiction in it.

Those who ask, however, must have the right sympathy or they will hear nothing.

HOW THE WARATAH GOT ITS HONEY

Krubi was the name of the beautiful black girl who became a waratah, and amongst the aborigines of the Burragorang Valley the name is only given to one girl of any tribe, of all its branches; and then only when the mother or the father has been reckoned to be very good looking, and the child is expected, therefore, to bear the same advantage (if advantage it is); so that not a baby girl can be christened Krubi until the former Krubi is dead.

Once upon a time, not long after the original Krubi had become a waratah plant, and her red cloak had made the brilliant hue of the flower, and only a very few other Krubis had ever been so named, a young lubra wife had determined that should she ever have a girl baby it must bear the coveted name. The living Krubi was very old, and already she had more than once failed to carry what her youngest child had put into her dilly-bag. That was the sign that her husband could leave her to the care of that youngest child, instead of staying back to aid her along.

The young wife wished for old Krubi's death very much. She was never far away when Krubi was being assisted by Warrindie, the youngest Of her family. But never did the good-looking lubra (Woolyan) so much as place her hand under Krubi's elbow.

But Krubi was wonderfully tenacious of life. She battled on.

She was relieved from all work. She had only to carry the dilly-bag when the tribe were moving, and they did not move much.

Woolyan grew very anxious. Her longing for the death of Krubi grew a passion. At last she determined to "bone" Krubi. No woman had ever done that. Only the men of her tribe were accustomed to kill by "boning."

So Woolyan picked out the fine shinbone of a big dingo, and she rubbed it with sand from the bed of the creek until it was white and smooth, and she hid it in her hair, awaiting the time when she could catch Krubi alone.

Many days sped by; several moons came and went.

Then the blacks determined to have a corroboree.

A good young man had been having private lessons in the things that were taught which Krubi and Woolyan and the other women were not permitted to see, and then came the great night.

It was very dark. A space had been cleared amongst the giant gum trees. But whilst it was still daylight the young women had chosen their places. Woolyan was delighted to see that Krubi was not well enough to take her place in the little march that the active old women made. So she got up from her place, and going back to Krubi, she hurriedly undid her hair that she had done up to hold the bone concealed, but before she could catch hold of it the thing fell to the ground.

Old Krubi saw it.

Then did old age give place to greater activity than youth possessed. With a bound and a yell Krubi jumped forward and stamped her foot on the death-dealing bone.

And Krubi's youngest bounded too. Woolyan was caught in a grip that she could not shake off, and blow after blow found her face and head and shoulders.

The corroboree was abandoned. The tribe surrounded the fighting women. But the chief demanded that the hubbub stop, and Krubi tell the cause of the trouble.

The sentence upon Woolyan was death. Before she was to die she "went bush." The beautiful waratahs were in bloom, and when Woolyan saw them all her false pride and hatred left her.

Kneeling beside a plant covered with the beautiful red flowers, her tears fell into them. They were tears of repentance. And as she wept her child was born.

She laid it at the foot of a waratah bush.

When the men who were to club her to death came and saw her they were filled with a great compassion.

So they sent for old Krubi.

There was a great reconciliation, and the tears of both women fell into the waratahs.

Woolyan's husband happened to smell the blooms and the scent was good. He plucked one separate flower, and the liquid within it crept into his fingers, He put them into his mouth, and, lo, the taste was very sweet!

So that day the waratah became a further source of comfort to the aborigines.

Sir James Smith wrote of it in 1793: "It is, moreover, a great favourite with the natives upon account of a rich honeyed juice which they sip from its flowers."

HOW THE WHITE WARATAH
BECAME RED

There is really a white waratah.

It occurs in New South Wales and in Tasmania.

It is not a distinct variety unless we consider a flower a variety simply because of its colour.

The white of New South Wales and that of Tasmania are *speciosissima* and *truncata* respectively, though the plants always bear blooms of the colour even though they are in close proximity to those of the usual glowing red.

In Tasmania white waratahs are in some profusion. In New South Wales pink ones have been found, and they surely have in some way been impregnated. Occasionally the white ones have had a creamy tinge at the base of the pistils and in such cases the flowers have obtained some food that is usually the property of the foliage.

In New South Wales white waratahs have been found, and may still be found at Mittagong, at Sherbrooke and on the Jamberoo Mountain.

The natives of Sherbrooke had a legend of the changing of the white to red, and perhaps this story shows that it was believed that the first were white and the change to red was a later effect. Of this we are not sure.

In the dense dark jungle there, a sleek and beautiful wonga pigeon lived. The rich soil in the gullied and sunken flats produced wonderful vegetation. Supplejacks and bloodwoods, cedars and monstrous turpentine! Great bushy lillypillies, overgrown myrtles, big laurels, towering eucalypts (*E. Consideniana*, the White Ash, *E. Smithii*, even *E. Sieberiana*, the Silver-top) shut out the daylight. Climbing plants grew there, with sweet smelling Sassafras (*Atherosperma moschatum*) and white Musk Daisy-bush (*Olearia argophylla*). In their shade the Flying Fox had camped for centuries unmolested.

Underfoot, the carpet of dark fallen leaves was feet thick. Down in there the horrible leech waved and swayed in his blind search for an animal to fasten upon in order to get his fill of blood, while the brown bottle-tick lost no time in detaching himself from his habitat to bury his proboscis in some unfortunate passer-by, in the same quest as the leech.

In there, too, were gorgeous parrots and pretty pigeons and bower-birds, and tits and wrens, and such a host of the feathered tribes as to make them seem like a moving mass of wings and swaying feathers.

Big brush wallabies softly hopped or curled in a tangled bower; the bush rat and the bandicoot peeked from their seclusion, and the native cat slunk about as only felines can.

There, in this deep, dank, dark, sweet-smelling Australian jungle stepped daintily and cooed quickly and loudly, that proud wonga.

Sailing serenely up above it all were the hawk and the eagle.

While the wonga remained indoors she was safe.

Up over the cliff, where the country was flat, the bush was rocky and open and dry. A dryer air pervaded, the ground was no carpet of fallen leaves, but a hot, sandy or gravelled area with but few fallen leaves, for there was no underscrub.

The hawk's piercing eye saw every move there.

The white waratah gazed skyward and felt dreadfully alone. All around the waratahs grew and perhaps they were red, and this one was the only one without colour, and it longed to be crimson like its neighbours of its own botanical genus.

The handsome wonga had lost her mate. Her grey spots glowed against their bed of white; her little pink legs strode briskly on, and she scratched and scratched and turned up insects and grubs, and she fed well.

But when her thoughts turned to companionship she discovered that she was lonely. So she coo-ed and coo-ed, ever more and more rapidly, and in higher and higher tones.

She stretched herself upon tip-toes and searched the jungle. She ceased to look for a surfeit of food, and she stepped on and on, always approaching the creek where beyond it the cliff rose, and above it was the open forest.

Up out there she would go!

So she opened her wings, and, heavy as she was, she rose with a great and ponderous flapping.

Increasing her speed, she swept by the trees over the brook, and up the cliff, alighting just at the foot of the white waratah.

Then she heard the call of her mate.

Foolish bird that she was!

He was still down in the darkened jungle.

His morning could not have been so successful as hers, or he was hungrier to start with, or perhaps he required more.

She opened her wings again.

Too late!

A rush through the air, like a streak of lightning or a shooting star!

Swish!

The hawk was down through the branchless space and upon the beautiful wonga beneath the white waratah.

But she was heavier than he reckoned.

There was a struggle, and in it a whirl of feathers-white and grey and green and golden-shimmered!

The hawk certainly rose, but he did not carry the wonga far.

The pigeon was torn, and her life was ebbing with the flow of her blood. Her last struggle was her release, and from a height of a few feet she wrenched herself free and fell upon the white waratah. Her little claws grasped the colourless pistils.

The eagle above all espied the hawk, and he had then to fight another battle in which he was the loser.

So the white waratah was stained with the blood of the wonga pigeon, and the bird, still clinging to the reddened pistils, died.

Later, the white waratah threw out its clusters of follicles, and they were streaked with red.

The seeds were streaked in the same way.

And all the plants that came from them bore flowers as red as waratahs could be.

But they had to wait for three years to know that.

Not so the parent bush. Always afterwards its flowers were white, and whenever the natives saw one such bloom they pricked their fingers and allowed their blood to stain it.

Therefore there are not many white waratahs in New South Wales.

THE SECOND KANGAROO STORY

Away in the Kowmung and around the rugged peaks under which lie the great lodes containing the silver of Yarranderie, roamed a tribe of blacks who have their own tale of the first kangaroo.

These people said that one day a woman hid from her husband. This man was a very clever food-getter. His unerring boomerang brought down every goanna. The boomerangs that he fashioned for playthings only, would spin away out on their farthest boundary, and would return and spin again and again above the head of the thrower before swiftly landing at his feet, and that which he made as a weapon and, of course, would not return, was always the heaviest and most deadly, whether in hunting or in war.

He could deftly turn over the porcupine and could not miss a bird if he tried to bring it down. Therefore the bag of his wife was always filled with goanna tails, with great porcupines and birds and grubs, though the wife herself got the grubs as well as the fern roots. The grubs were the beautiful white ones that lie in interstices in old logs and are called "nuttoo."

The first kangaroo was said to be a great beast and was not innocent of eating small black children. Should a picaninny endeavour to crawl away from its rug or its sheet of bark its mother always threatened it with the calling of the giant kangaroo.

Now the heavily-laden wife one day rebelled. She threw away the heavy bag and ran off. She was fleet of foot, too, for no one could catch her.

Around that part of the country are many swampy patches, and these patches are mostly densely wooded with the *Melaleuca Maideni* and were similarly overgrown in the far-off days of the first kangaroo.

The fugitive wife hid behind the trunk of one of the biggest of these trees. Its bark is white, and in broad patches, soft and paper-like and irregular. It will peel off in huge scales.

Her husband often ran close to her, and she had to be very, very quick in her darting from the cover, and racing on.

Days went by and still she was not caught. But she was growing tired, and she began to think that carrying a heavy bag of tainted flesh was not so terrible a task as that of playing the grim game of hide and seek for life, in which she was obliged now to indulge continually.

Had she not been one of the women who had learned secrets that were supposed only to be possessed by the men, she would never have dared to rebel. If things came to the worst she could invoke the aid of the spirit, and something would happen in her favour. She knew where the necessary clay was to be found. The only trouble was that she was unaware of the whereabouts of her people. However, she chanced everything, and scaling the precipitous side of the mount she saw the smoke from the camp fire.

She was overjoyed to perceive that it was away towards the mountain now called "Werong," whereas when she escaped it was under "Alum Rocks." And between her and Alum Rocks was a deposit of red, and yellow, and white pipeclay. Thither she went, and soon she was correctly marked, and she even stuck the wild cotton in the lines of the clay to make sure that she would get the aid she needed.

By that time it was night, and she slept.

In the morning food came to her. The nuttoo grub poked its head from the trunk of the grass tree, and she had no difficulty in drawing him right out; and, roasted, he was very sweet. The taste of the nuttoo made her long for the grub that may nearly always be found in wattles.

It is well known that a very large number of very destructive insects inhabit wattles. The coolibah, too, is another host for pest grubs. And wattle and coolibahs grew in plenty, therefore in less than two hours she had collected a bagful, and then she sought a place to make another fire.

This fire was her undoing. The smoke was observed by her husband. He had never ceased to watch and to search for her.

With all his cunning he approached the little blue curling threads.

The woman was by no means unmindful. Her ears were alert, and distinctly she detected the distant crack of the broken twig, and the rustle o' disturbed dead leaves. The woman called upon the spirit, beating her breasts the while. Between her and the stealthily creeping man was a tea-tree stump. The top had been torn out by a gale and lay dead on the ground. She crept to it, and straightening up she clasped her arms around it, beseeching the spirit at the same time to protect and guide her.

The tea-tree stump became animated. It pulsed with life. It had almost parted from its roots before, for it was long since the branched top had been wrenched from it.

The man saw it quite plainly. It was only a tea-tree stump. The great flakes of bark were quite plain to him.

Therefore he did not watch it particularly. On he came until he could see the smouldering fire, and his nostrils told him of the cooking meal. There was no sign of his wife.

Well, he thought, never mind, this time. He would eat her meal and then he would spy out her tracks and follow her.

He passed within a few yards of the tea-tree stump, and just as he was quite off his guard and was about to begin the meal, the stump bounded off. He threw a glance up to it. Surprise held him paralysed. There, clinging to the stump as it went, was his wife.

He caught a glimpse of the white lines of the sign, and he gave up the idea of following.

Therefore ever since that time it is hard to tell a kangaroo from a stump. As he stands still in the bush one can easily imagine the black woman, plastered with clay and wild cotton, on his back. The dark forepaws of the kangaroo are her arms. His dark back is her body. His dark head is her face. But his white shaggy front is the ti-tree stump.

His one fault is his desire for black babies, and that was born of the woman who caused his being. Some believed that he ate them, but others deny that, and so they say it will never be known.

Even if not believed, the black mothers frightened their children by saying that he did.

THE DIANELLA BERRY

We have given the rush with the pretty blue berries its name after the Goddess of the Woods - Diana - the hunter's deity. And it is strange but true that the aborigines had an idea much the same. They said that the plant at one time in the alcheringa was the hair of a certain woman who lived deep in the bush.

She had some sisters, however, and they lived sometimes in the forests and sometimes in the air for their other home was in the great cumulus clouds that lie lazily above the sea.

The one who lived in the bush only, had for a husband a mighty hunter whose voice was so loud that when he spoke angrily every animal and bird and even insect and reptile fled from that part of the country and did not return for a very long, time.

The woman was always most grieved when she saw the animals that she loved flying in fear, and one day when her husband had been especially angry one little bird grew too tired to fly far and it came to her for help. Her hair was at that time very luxuriant and she took the little bird and hid it in it.

After that many birds found the same sanctuary under similar circumstances and at last the number was so great that it was impossible for them all to be hidden. One bird - the woodpecker - begged to be allowed to leave and to try his luck by hiding under the loose bark of a big tree. This place was not secure, and when the angry man saw him there with part of his body showing, he threw his spear. It missed, but was so close as to make the woodpecker hop sharply further up. Another spear and then another were thrown, each one causing the frightened bird to jump one more step upwards.

The man's anger waned; his arm grew tired: he lay down to sleep. The bird flew to the woman and plucked one hair from her head. This he hid, hoping that the next time that the big hunter was angry and roared the hair would be enough to cover, not one woodpecker only, but the whole woodpecker family.

It is noticed that woodpeckers to this day hop up and up the trunks of trees and the blacks say that they are looking for a place to hide from the wrath of a forest giant. They listen intently and strain their ears to catch the sound of the roaring.

We know that the birds are simply looking for food, and some of us believe that the aborigines know this quite well, only feigning to think that it is for any other purpose. Perhaps they think the tale is too pretty to lose.

Next time that the hunter was angry and threatening, the woodpecker tried his plan. He flew to the place where he had hidden the strand of hair, and he found that he could be covered with it by winding it around himself until none was left hanging. Other birds saw the plan and followed it.

The time came when the woman had but little hair left. But rain fell where the hairs were put and warm sun shone on the places and the hairs grew and flowers came upon them all and afterwards berries formed.

It was no longer necessary for the birds and the animals to flee far to escape the wrath of the husband of their benefactor.

They only had to quickly haste to one cluster of growing hairs and snuggle down in amongst them and they were quite hidden.

But the day came when a jealous sister came down from the cumulus cloud. She told the man and he declared that he would find every one of those clusters and destroy them. The sister gave directions to the rest of the family still up in the sky that they were to keep their clouds away from the place so that no more rain could fall and the hairs would no longer grow. She saw that the wife was now denuded of hair and she wanted to please the husband and thought that no more could ever be seen after those growing ones were destroyed.

But the berries had fallen and lay covered by the now dry soil. The clusters of hairs did die, and the earth suffered from a great drought.

Then the man grew more and more sullen and was more and

more often dreadfully angry. His wife had gone away from him. The birds had hidden her and with their wings they protected her, and the cloud sister lived in her place.

She no longer spoke to those still in the sky. They heard of her treachery and they did not want to speak to her. They at last determined to no longer heed her request to keep away from that place and they came again and they brought the lightning and the thunder with them. They poured their rain down upon the earth and every little blue berry gave birth to another hair that took root and became a plant.

The rain kept on longer than ever before and there was a great flood, but not any of these hair rushes was destroyed. To-day they grow where the ground is wettest, as well as in dryer parts.

Aboriginal women of all the east coast of Australia know this story and they believe it, and because they think that the spirit of the woman who loved birds and animals is still in the dianella rush they like that plant best for the weaving of baskets and mats.

HOW THE PISTILS OF THE
WARATAH BECAME FIRM

Of all the flowers in our Australia one which was most revered by the blacks (in fact the only one so far as we know) was the watarah. No other flower was ever sufficiently noticed by them to be plucked and given, or shown, to whites, with a sense of gratitude for a good done to them.

There was a time, say the natives of the Burragorang Valley, when the waratah was not as we see it to-day. The pistils were soft and downy, and when the wind blew they fell off and floated away like the thistledown.

It all happened at a corroboree.

Wantaba and Wirrawaa were rivals for a maiden. Both men knew that he who sprang the highest in play, he who wielded the longest spear, and above all, he who went out alone into the dark and brought back the finest 'possum or the prettiest flower plucked in the dark of night, would win the girl.

The hated and feared tribe that came over the hills from the swampy country at the base of the great unscalable mountain had twice been seen trespassing on the Burragorang side of the waterfall, and two corroborees had been held so that the young men who had never had a fight might be shown how to hurl a spear and how to crouch, and how to wield the millah, and dodge a blow, and also how to feign death if the enemy hit hard enough and proved to be too strong.

The warriors, old and new, sallied out, and climbed to the top of the Dividing Range. There they sat around little pools of rain water that the tiny basins in the rocks held, and rubbed and rubbed their stone axes and spearheads, and chanted song after song, deriding the wrongdoers of the other tribe, until at last one of them yelled to know what all the din was about.

The answer was a hurled spear. Wantaba was anxious to show what he could do, and he threw the spear that had taken him many days to fashion. Wirrawaa was more cautious. Plucking a waratah, which was then only a soft cluster of pollen like a wattle, he held it before his face while he took a careful aim at the seeming valiant enemy. He moved carefully forward, crouching the while just as old Wollayabba had done at the corroboree in which he was the teacher of the warlike arts, and knowing that by the time he was near enough to be sure of killing the foe and recovering, too, the spear that he would soon fling, many others of the opposing force would be collected at the spot.

He drew nearer the edge of the ridge, step by step, and then came a puff of wind. The fluff of the flower blew back into his eyes, and just then came a spear from the throwing stick of one of the foes.

Crack! It caught Wirrawaa fairly on the forehead, and down be went like a stone.

That was the signal for a rush. Fighting men of both sides had clustered in rear of their companions, and now came the deciding clash. Down below on the sides of the ridge and on the top of another the women and children waited and watched and listened. Some could see the battle, some were too frightened to look, and some were not allowed to see what was going on. They could all know by the nearness of the noise which side was giving way, and the Burragorang women grew much afraid. They gathered up their mats and bags, for the sound of the fighting grew ever louder.

Their men were being fought back. There were some bark shields lying handy, and two or three of the girls who had lovers fighting up on the hill grabbed them and rushed nearer to the fray. Wantaba, who had thrown the first spear was still in the battle line. Just as the girls with the shields came in sight, Wantaba received a mighty blow from a kurri, as the knobbed fighting-club was called.

He turned and fled. Catching sight of the young woman for whom he and the fallen Wirrawaa strove he saw that she was holding out a bark shield for him, and he sped to her.

But she asked for Wirrawaa. Wantaba pointed to his own head and then to a point in the midst of the struggling warriors and returned to the fray. The girl was afraid now that he would be killed like Wirrawaa, so calling to Wantaba she too rushed into the fight, and just in time.

Many of her people had thrown down their clubs. Most of them were either killed or badly injured.

But when the survivors saw a woman laying about her with an old stick, and warding off blows with a man's huge bark shield, they picked up their weapons again and fought more determinedly than ever.

They won, and the trespassing blacks were driven far into their own territory.

Upon the return of the pursuers to the scene of the fight a procession was formed in which were a few young women, and this was an unprecedented thing. There was a triumphal march back to the camp and the place was cleared for another corroboree.

Wantaba was asked to tell his story and, dressed for the part in his proper war colours, he acted it and pointed out the girl who had fought and acclaimed her the real conqueror.

Then at the end of this recital and this portrayal the women were all sent into thick scrub, and Wantaba was inducted into the mysteries of the marriage state.

But the ceremony had to be postponed for the girl was not to be found. She had disappeared and no one had seen her going. When daylight came the whole tribe engaged in the search, for it was believed that she could not possibly have gone far, and it was feared that she had received some hurt.

She had entered again into the domain of man, for she had communed with the god of her totem. She had asked that Wirrawaa be allowed to come back from the spirit world to her. She had taken a waratah and had shown how the fluffy bloom had succumbed to the blowing of the wind and had proved no protection to a fighting man. And her prayer was answered.

Wirrawaa came back, though a much changed man. His skin was white and the eyes that before were nearly black were now sightless and blue.

And he had a strange power. He could alter the form of trees and change their flowers. As a protection to any other fighting men who might pluck a flower or a plant when going into battle, he caused spikes and thorns to grow upon many trees and he changed many soft flowers into hard ones. The waratah became the firmest of all.

The prickly hakea now prevents any one from pushing through it. Smilax and many other vines produced such thorns and prickles that they were a sufficient guard to any lands.

For a long time it was believed that no spear would go through a waratah flower, and many blacks would ask white men to put one up and let someone hurl a dart or a spear and it would not go through. So much faith was placed in that, that many men would not go into battle without a waratah if they were in flower at the time of the quarrel.

WHAT MAKES THE WAVES

Arrilla was of the Kamilaroi.

He lived principally on the coast, not far from our present village of Coal Cliff-between that and Stanwell Park.

Perhaps he was not any real individual, but only a type-creation. Be that as it may, all that is ascribed to him in this legend is what happened under the circumstances delineated. The story was told as being of one particular man, and yet there is that in the telling of it that seems to indicate a wish to show tradition rather than tell of the actual doings of one person.

He was the cleverest of his tribe.

He was not afraid of the sea.

He roamed as he willed over his country, and even when enemies appeared on the top of the range and a hurried council was called by the King, Arrilla did not hasten to obey the summons if he happened to be studying the inhabitants of the sea, or the denizens of the creeks that came clattering down the slopes and spread out into beautiful lagoons on the beach.

For his country is a narrow strip of sub-tropical country, backed by a jungled range with ironstone scarps for its topmost face scarred by cold creeks and edged by bold promontories and yellow scalloped beaches that bound the limitless expanse of Pacific Ocean.

He never dared to remain away from a summoned council altogether.

And one morning when the sun shone calmly and clearly down through the blue, and the mountain was purpled, and the lower slopes were deep green and dark with the jungle, and the strip of undulating land that lay between it and the beach was bright with the semi-tropical verdure such as the tamarind, and the palms (*Archontophoenix* and *Livistona*) and the giant Alsophila ferns (*Cooperi* and *australis*) - and the promontories stood with their shaggy *westringias* and *hibbertias* and *hardenbergias* and white button-flowers all aglow, staring, staring, staring out over the blue lazy ocean, and casting blue and purple shadows across the yellow sand of the beach, even reaching to the masses of white foam that were swept ashore, when the little breakers were dashed to pieces, the enemy was seen on the top, above the dark wall of ironstone, right out on the edge, waving spears, and he was heard shouting to the family of Arrilla down on the beach.

The voice carried far.

Aborigines could be heard at a distance of seven miles.

They made hollows with their hands, and the coo-ee that rang through them was a wonderfully penetrating and floating call.

The King was young.

It was not long since his father was laid in the shallow grave that was scooped out in a grass-grown sandhill.

The spears were buried with him.

They put him sitting with his face towards the mountain and his knees doubled up to his chin and his arms crossed over his stomach.

His three wives still sat and beat their breasts in grief, and the blood that ran from the cuts they made in their thighs was dried on their legs, for they would not wash it off for three moons.

The young King was as stern as his father had been.

He was as straight as a rush, too, and he was fleet and wary.

Above all, he was determined.

So when Arrilla delayed he ordered two strong men to go to the lagoon and seize him.

Now Arrilla was cunning.

He had practised his subtleties on the old King, and that is why he was allowed to respond to a summons as unhurriedly as he wished.

Arrilla asked to be allowed to speak, and the permission being given, he drew himself erect and waited until he saw that the expectancy of the warriors of the family was beginning to make them impatient.

Then he pointed to the highest spot on the range. He told them that in his wanderings there he had seen a spirit. The spirit was not friendly to him, but would be good to any stranger who came over the range at that point. He said that the enemy that then stood on the very spot was receiving his courage from that spirit and there was only one way to overcome it.

It was not by an organised battle. It was by strategy, and he was the only fighting man of the family who possessed the cunning.

And in that way Arrilla tried to palliate the King and to escape the opprobrium that always attached itself to those who disobeyed or were dilatory in answering a call to the councils or an order of the King.

But this time the King was not convinced. He said that the meeting was to be adjourned until night came, and then the further evidence of Arrilla would be taken. There was, he said, no immediate danger from the enemy above. If he were prepared to fight he would have been down before, said the King. He was only seeking to make the people below too angry to fight, and then he might bring his forces down and get the gain he was after.

So the meeting broke up. Arrilla was free. That much he had gained he knew, for he saw very plainly that though he had been always before successful in placating the King, this time he was in deep disfavour and perhaps would be punished.

He had succeeded in making his fellows think he had had communion with a spirit on the top of the range, and with them that belief gave him a great prestige. All aborigines were vain and fond of power, and in that they were no very great amount different from white people.

Arrilla went to the wurley of his wife, and for a little while he played with his two children.

Then he looked into the dilly-bag, and finding that there was not much in it, he decided to go out in search of some food. He had noticed women putting things within reach of his wife, but he had been too busy with his own interests to see that his larder was so empty.

Taking up a spear and a shield he strode into the scrub. There was, at first, a thick tangle of boronia - *Boronia mollis* - and its scent was not pleasant to him. Bracken fern, rank and tall, *Chorizema* and snake vine, *Bauera* with the always blooming pink flowerets, and *Tetratheca*, with the layer of tangled twigs, made the going difficult. Prickly wild raspberries made the way even more hard for him. Then he entered the dark jungle itself. Its edge was a mass of myrtles interwoven with the *rubus* and flowering *tecoma* and *clematis*. These vines lay thick on the top of lantana, and through them grew up the Lillypilli and *Rapanea* and the fluffy-flowered *Callicoma*. Native pear trees (*Xylomelum pyriforme*) with their wooden fruit and unpleasant odour, and the *Goodenia ovata* with its dark serrated leaves and yellow flowers and the *Pittosporum* and Sassafras were all clasped together and held close by native jasmine, and up through it all the cabbage and bangalow palms and the Eucalyptus *microcorys* or tallow wood and the Swamp Mahogany or *robusta* of the eucalyptus genus stood into the humid air.

Big cold boulders were lying under the deep shade of the scrub and ferns and the clustered true and false sarsaparilla, and they were covered with moss and lichen, and attached to them were *dendrobiums* and big *aspleniums* or bird's-nest fern.

It was always dark in there.

The lyre-bird darted under the thick moss and the carpet of *Randia* and tiny wild violets overlaid with the tough and thick-leaved *Smilax australis*.

Its nest was placed on a flat ledge of the biggest rock and it had in it a furry youngster that sat as still as the rock itself, its eye of black fire fully taking in the cautious Arrilla.

Right in front the mountain reared, still clothed with the jungle, with giant rocks fast to the sides, and the vines, especially the tough monkey vines, clinging to big gums - the turpentine, the woolly-butt, and the spotted gum and the wild fig with its mass of roots between which men could hide and wallabies often had their lairs.

Arrilla sought the wallaby. The rufus-necked scrub variety was in plenty here. Arrilla only had to stand still with poised spear and an unsuspecting marsupial hopped into view.

"Swish"!

It was like a dart of lightning.

Then Arrilla "twooped" like a beautiful wonga pigeon, and he whistled like the king parrot, and those birds came to what they supposed was a calling mate.

He very soon had a fine collection of game for his food and the meat of his family. He was a snake man and only reptiles were tabu to him.

It grew night again.

The rest of his people were scattered about on the clearer and lighter land, nearer the beach-some idling and some fashioning weapons. Some indeed were making cradles, but not on rockers as are our cradles. They had strings attached and could be fastened round the neck of the mother.

A few had made a poison from the acacia for their fishing, and yet others were wading in pools in the rocks seeking mussels and shell-fish.

Beyond, the lazy sea just heaved and sparkled and sent its messengers of breakers to be broken on the sand.

By this time a black band had spread along the horizon, for night was approaching.

What had become of the gesticulating blackfellow on top of the range no one knew.

No cooking fires were lighted. Little heaps of sticks lay about-all gathered by the fathers and the children. Suitable stones were collected too, but the order had gone out that everyone must eat either raw or cold food, and a big council would be held on the low, flat, grassy patch down near the lagoon.

Only after nightfall did the sea begin to moan.

The little crash of the breaking waves in the daytime was quite cheerful, but in the darkness it seemed to ring with a different tone-one of sadness and pessimism.

The council sat in the dark. Only the fighting men and the priests were in it after all.

Arrilla was there.

The discussion did not last long, and it all centred upon the tale that Arrilla had told.

He was a frightened Arrilla when he found that he was expected to climb to the highest point of the range and ask questions of the spirit to whom he said he had spoken.

He dared not disobey.

When the meeting was over and the men had retired to their wurlies and their families, Arrilla sat for a long time arranging in his mind how he would proceed as soon as it was light.

He determined not to go by the way he had gone before. He would go a long way round.

He knew of a gully up which it was easy to climb and which would allow him to approach the enemy by a flanking manoeuvre, and then he could spy upon him and perhaps use his spear.

So in the morning he said "good-bye" to his wife, and having received a sacred stone from the priest for placing in his hair above his ear for good luck, he again crossed through the boronia and *leptospermum* and bracken undergrowth, and entered the jungle. He went to the rock on which was the lyre-bird's nest, and then turning to the right he passed close to a giant nettle tree and a *Stenocarpus*, and that way the going was easy. He was still under the big trees and hidden from anyone's sight unless someone were very close.

The scent of the *dendrobiums* came to him, and as he passed lilly-pillies he broke off a few clusters of the white and juicy fruit and ate them. He picked up ripe and luscious black apples, and here and there he gathered the little red berries of the *Rubus parvifolius*. The wild raspberry he made a detour for, but it was not growing in that part. Occasionally he tore up a leaf from the bird's-nest fern and at the end there is a crisp and succulent part which he chewed.

He reached the upper part of the creek that formed the lagoon down below on the beach, and as he was gradually ascending the lower slope and using the maximum of precaution, he came to a spot high on the mountain side from which he could look out through the branches and over the heads of the tall shrubs and high gums to the sea.

The sun was well up and the morning was becoming warm. The sea was still lazy though a little glitter on its surface showed that it was under a disturbance, slight enough, but discernible.

Then he turned his back to that view and the climb proper commenced. It was steep. He hoisted himself by grasping the stems of the *callicomas* and the *rapaneas* and the myrtles that grew sparsely here, and sometimes he was lucky enough to find a monkey vine hanging to a tree and that gave him a splendid lift. Though he was somewhat afraid of his errand and quite alone, he was not anxious to lose time; yet the temptation to swing on a monkey vine was too strong, and finding one that had a big loose bight in it he seized it and pushed himself off with his feet. Out he swung over the steep side and above the undergrowth and through the lesser limbs of the *Pittosporum* that grew just beneath, and then he had a clear and uninterrupted sight of the country at the base, and of the beach and the sea. The vine gave a little twist and returned, and the swing was exhilarating.

But he only did it once, and letting the vine go he faced the escarpment and went on with his climb. He secured precarious footing on the stones and exposed roots and in the moss. Sometimes a loosened stone went bounding and crashing down until it struck the foot of a tree and lodged there.

Arrilla now looked up. He had reached a spot where the big trees did not grow, and the only verdure was rock fern and *dianella* rush with its tiny blue and yellow flowers and its blue fruit.

Above him the blue sky was unclouded and a great lazy sea-eagle floated serenely.

He had disturbed many birds in his climb. The coach-whip had darted from him. The wonga pigeon and the little brown fantail and the woodpeckers and the honey-eaters and the diamond sparrows and white-eyes and silver-eyes all had paused to watch him go by. Satin birds and catbirds and parrots sat in the branches or darted through them as he passed under, and in the wild fig-trees the beautiful flock and topknot pigeons clattered and scrambled for fruit.

A small colony of flying foxes hung like a giant swarm of bees in a fire-tree, but Arrilla did not see them. This fire-tree is a *Brachychiton*, and it is of the same genus as the Queensland bottletree. It sheds its leaves and its brilliant flamelike flowers cover the twigs and blaze out before any of the new season's leaves come. It is rightly named "fire-tree," though some people call it "flame-tree," and apply this name also to the *Erythrina* or coral tree of Queensland.

He was in the narrow cleft, between the sides of which the water raced in rain-time, and he was near to the top.

When reached it, and before he had climbed over the ledge, he was in a bracing upper air. The verdure, he could see as he peered, was different. The *Epacris* and the *Boronia pinnata* and *Boronia serrulata*, and also Star-hair made a pink carpet.

Arrilla was out of breath and perspiring when he heaved himself over and stood upright in that upper air with its scents of new flowers.

On damp and mossy and heathy patches the *Blandfordia* bloomed. On drier parts the false sarsaparilla or *Hardenbergia monophylla* clambered over the stones and boulders and clefts, and hung its blooms in purple clusters.

Here and there a big yellow *Podolepis acuminata* glowed and the white fur from the stems was detached and lay on the ground.

Box-trees - the Eucalyptus bicolor - and stunted *Banksia serrata*, and *Callistemon lanceolatus* tried to find sustenance.

Mustering all his caution Arrilla advanced along the edge of the mountain. Heath abounded, hard rock-fern clustered thickly, stunted *callitris* scrub, *Olearia* or mountain musk dwarfed eucalypts, honey-flower or *Lambertia formosa*, little casuarinas, wild currants, or *Leucopogon richei* and bracken fern, were matted with *kennedya*, well out in crimson and black flowers, and here and there rising through them stood the gorgeous crimson waratah.

As Arrilla quietly crept along the edge he could see down over the verdure to his people near the beach, and he noticed that many were looking anxiously in the direction of the point on which he had seen the enemy native the day before.

He had all their love for the representative flower of his race - the waratah - and he plucked one in order to render himself immune from fire should that occur.

Suddenly he cast himself into a rigid statuesque figure of a man.

He heard the breaking of twigs and the footfall of someone. He moved not a muscle. His spears were in the hand that held the shield.

The noise ceased.

Then the air darkened. There were no clouds, but a great deep shade spread all over the earth.

Arrilla looked to the sun.

It was disappearing.

He grew mightily afraid.

He had almost persuaded himself that he really had spoken some time or other to a spirit up there, and this terrible fading out of the sunlight came to show that he was even then trespassing on the country of it. The place surely was sanctuary and tabu.

So making the sign with his hand that he had seen the priests make he softly whispered a magic word.

The strange shade grew rapidly deeper and then Arrilla became conscious that another aborigine was standing just as frightened as he and was looking at him fixedly.

Arrilla made a friendly sign and the other advanced. He was an utter stranger but his language was much like Arrilla's. They could well understand one another.

He told Arrilla that he was in country strange to him, and his story was a long one. He had never before seen the sea, and he did not know what it was. He believed it to be a great sky, and beyond it there was, a very bad country. He said that the sky had fallen down and that it was slowly creeping on and on and eventually would cover the whole world. In his country he had heard some such tale about it. It was that a great ancestor had left the earth and had gone up into the sky. He went so fast that he drove right through it and he had seen the very bad country that is beyond it. He tried to return but the hole that he had made was closed up. Yet he did not give up hope, and by beating upon it he loosened it and it fell. It had as much life as a man, and it very much wanted to return from whence it had fallen. The ancestor was always with it, floating upon it. And when it tried to rise up to return the ancestor beat it back and it could do nothing but sink down and break itself on the beach. However, it was surely growing and spreading, and the time must come when it would cover the earth.

He had heard all these things and he had determined to see for himself, and that is why he had made the journey in the direction his people had pointed out as the one where the great sky lay.

Arrilla was delighted to hear this story. Though he had been born near the sea and lived there all his life he had no story of what it is, nor how it comes to be there, nor why the waves beat on the shore.

He advised the strange man to wait until he had gone back and communicated the news to his people, and said that when the signal fire was made he might come down and be received by the King. But Arrilla told him to say that a spirit gave him all this information about the sea and the waves, and that while it was being told Arrilla was present.

Both forgot their fears of the strange darkness that had come over, and down below his people still wondered what had caused it. They thought it was because Arrilla had met the spirit and was talking to it, and as the shade passed and the sun came out bright again and the gladness that is usual to the sunshine spread again all were in high glee. There was nothing wrong, they said, and Arrilla would return with news and the spirit he had seen and spoken with would assist them if they had to fight with any trespassing tribe or family group.

Soon after Arrilla joined his people again, having come down the way he went up, and he told the story of the sea as he had heard it from the stranger, though he said it was told him by the spirit.

Fires were lighted, and when the man came to them he said he was very hungry, and he told the story just as Arrilla had.

A wife was found for him from amongst the women-girls and he lived there for the rest of his days with that family.

The sea grew rough when the wind blew, and he said that he had heard that that was the impatience of the sea. It was angry and impatient because of the great delay occasioned by the ancestor who refused to let it go back to where it had fallen from.

The roar is the voice of the ancestor who always refuses to go back. When the calm came again it was because the sea was worn out and very tired, but nothing could stop it from ever creeping further and further over the land. The winds, be said, were the spirit friends of the sea, and they tried to assist it to regain the place that it had lost.

The Kamilaroi people always believed that the day would come when the sky would go back and the earth would be quite dry and life could not exist, but they were not afraid, for they said that the day was yet a long way off.

AT LOW TIDE

This is a story of, in part, the coming of white men to Australia.

Whether it is wholly true or not does not, perhaps, matter much.

It is true this far - that since the earliest times the aborigines did believe that a black man was taken by a great white spirit and he became the ancestor of the great white race. It was thought that this black man was so favoured by the god that he took him to his own realm, and that occasionally, at times remote from one another, some aborigine nearly as much favoured, was allowed to penetrate after death into the country of this white race and become white like the ones there, and then come back for a time to his people.

So we have many accounts of white people being taken to the hearts of the blacks just because they thought that perhaps those whites were the favoured blacks who came back.

Often a sear on the white man was the recognised mark; sometimes it was a peculiarity of hair; sometimes an uncommon walk, and sometimes there was some likeness in facial features. The blacks were all very quick to notice such things.

There are many stories of kindnesses done by the blacks at times when the white was powerless, and it is a fact that the traits of human character that make for benevolence and charity were pronounced in the autochonous inhabitants of this country.

All over Australia men and women watched for the return of the man who was taken to be the ancestor of a white race. On the great plains the vantage points were trees, but if there were an outstanding rocky eminence periodical pilgrimages were made to it. On the highlands the place was always a cool gully with moss and fern-grown sides, while on the coast it was always the highest of a line of sand-dunes or the top of a rock-bound promontory.

That white morning away back in the thousands of years ago that brought Allambee from his gunyah (he was called Allambee because he was slow in his movements), blinking at the sun that was just crawling up from beyond the edge of the sea, was just the same as the many white mornings that brought me out of my tent to look at the same sun steadily rising from beyond the horizon down on the New South Wales Coast, somewhere in the mists of my past.

But in Allambee's days there were different things everywhere. Whether of the animal world or the plant world or of the spirit world the aborigines were not clear, and from what they said, I believe that it was of the spirit world, for their belief in magic from above nature, and the supernatural in all things, was pathetically great.

The sky became brilliant. The sea was whitey-grey with specks of flashing silver coming from the sun to a wide mark just behind the breakers. These specks danced like shaking beads.

Away to the north the sea was calm and flat and still and light blue; away to the south it was just as calm and flat but a little bluer. The horizon was level and clear and sharp. The breakers were very lazy. They just reared up and broke in white foam and fell and came on and in. When they reached the beach they slipped in lines of tiny foam and turned and faded out. The beach was yellow and massed with shells and dry cuttlefish and a few old water-smoothed logs lay about on the sand. An irregular line of *mesembryanthemum* and marram-covered dunes stood then, and Xerotes rush with the pebbly and spikey flowers forbade unwary trampling. Big old gnarled *Banksia serrata* leaned over bowing to the sea, and the underscrub was *leptospermum* and bracken fern with a tangle of *hibbertia* and *smilax* and *hardenbergias*.

It was a clear patch that sloped to a wide rushy lagoon, and back of it all the flat-sided and sheer and dense-clad range.

Now, of this beauty all is gone but the sea and the sky, for white man is the despoiler of nature. The range is made bare. The lagoon is dried up. The banksias and the ferns and the bushes are all gone. The sand dunes are all torn away, and the shells are trampled and broken. The dust of civilisation and the dirt of coal mines and the dazing noise of industry - the, after all, useless industry - of white man, vilify the air.

When white men came the land was as Allambee saw it and as it had been for the ages. Whatever difference occurred was the difference of evolution, not of revolution. A flat patch of rock to the southwards that was edged with green mosses and sprays of seaweed caught the breakers and the mosses were sparkled and the seaweed swung with the water as it receded. When the tide was low and the waves just murmured and the seagulls swept the surface with their sharp wings there was a wide, low slope of beach.

Allambee walked amongst the sleeping people and stood on the sand dunes.

He saw a strange sight. A white man sat on the sea over against the flat patch of rock. He was very big.

He had flowing hair and a big mass of beard and his eyes could be seen even at a great distance. And in his hand he held a long spear.

Allambee had never seen such a spear before. He had never seen anything like this sight, for the man was huge and bright and white, and all about and belonging to this apparition was the same-huge and bright and white.

At first he was very frightened.

The sun came high up and the sparkling flashes became less and less and the white morning became blue and a little breeze sprang up in the north-east and came on in little pulses across the sea and stirred the leaves of the banksias.

The people moved and dogs stretched themselves and yawned.

Allambee forgot his fears and determined to go across to the rocks to see the big man who sat on the sea. He wanted to talk to him. The great stranger said that he had come to choose a good man to go with him to the place from whence he had come, for a king was wanted there to become an ancestor and to cause a race of people to come to inhabit the land and make it grow the beautiful things that were on other parts of the coast, especially that part which we call Illawarra. He asked Allambee if he would go, and though Allambee thought of his wife and his children and his people, he thought, too, that it would be fine to be a king, and what is so much better, an ancestor, so he consented to go. But he must return to the camp and have just one last look at those whom he really loved. He found his wife and his little brown baby on the sand dunes just where he had stood when he saw the big man out on the water. Others of the family group by this time were astir, and were either preparing food and weapons, or were trying to decide where they would hunt during the day. Many women were seated at fires, and watching to see the round stones become heated enough to use for baking meat and fish. Others were idly jabbing their digging sticks into the grass. The rest were either patting the dogs or just standing awaiting orders. Children were playing about-some in the lagoon and some on the sandy patches or amongst the green grass.

Some men were busy extracting the tough sinews from wallabies' legs to use as tying-string and binding their stone axes in the handles. Others were applying themselves to the cooking and the fashioning of weapons, as I have written.

None had gone to the beach. Only Allambee's wife had reached the sand-dunes, and there she sat awaiting her husband.

When he came he told her what had happened. She looked across to the rocks but she could see no man at all. She grew very much afraid, for she thought that if Allambee had seen any such thing he must be what the Scotch call "fey." So she said nothing, and taking her child close to her she rose simply, but with much trepidation and inward weakness, and went back to the camp.

Allambee followed.

All the people could see that something had occurred to Allambee, and the wife whispered that it was magical and no one spoke to him. They were afraid that he perhaps possessed magic power and that he might use it to their detriment or at least disadvantage.

So Allambee silently passed out from the people and going down to the rocks he waded into the water. Many of the family group went as far as the dunes and from there they watched. The principal watcher was his wife.

During many days that followed she went out there, and though other women tried to comfort her she would not be comforted. Her husband was not dead, therefore she did not wear the white clay that was usual, and that, being a dress of some sort, was, even in their distress because of the loss of a husband, a source of satisfaction. She did her work. She entered into the preparing of the food just as before. She tended her children. When the women went to the rocks either to the north or to the south to assist in the catching of crustaceans or the spearing of swimming fish or the trapping of eels, she went too. She made ropes of fur and bags of rushes and sea-grass, and she watched the black under her baby's skin gradually spreading over his little body, but in it all- during all her days, and while she was awake at night, she waited and longed for her husband.

She believed that one day he would come back and she would know him.

Then came the time when the king ordered the people to go to another part of the coast. While they were wending their way along the beach they came to a place where a creek spread itself out on the sand, and only a narrow bar separated it from the water of the sea.

Allambee's wife was the first to essay to pass along the bar. It was of sodden sand, and underneath that there was much soft and rotted weed. She sank. The sand was a patch of treacherous quicksand. Allambee's little boy was left without either father or mother. He was cared for by some of his relatives, for all those people whom Allambee, by the rules of his race, might have married were considered as much mother as the real mother, and Allambee's brothers as well as those brothers of the women he could have taken to wife were uncles, so no orphan could ever be without relatives. When he grew up he became a priest and he thought that his father was taken by a spirit for some great work and that his mother had joined him. This belief was shared by the people and Allambee's son was looked upon with more awe than reverence. He was under instruction for many months but the day came when he was accredited, and after that his ministrations were accepted and he grew to be of great importance. The people had moved back and forth many times. He knew all the story of his father, and every time that the camp was back near those flat rocks he spent many mornings on the sand-dunes gazing out to sea and hoping to find his father coming back with the great white spirit with whom he had gone away.

When again the tide was full and the rocks were covered and the breakers dashed against the cliffs and the beach was under water he did not bother to look. If the storm blew and the rain fell, and the wind lashed the leaves of the banksias and twirled the bushes and the streamers of marram that grew on the sandhills he thought it was no time to watch, for then the sea was very rough and no one, not even a spirit, could walk on it.

His day at last passed away and he went out into the beyond and his people buried him in the sand. All the rest of the people who died were buried in the shallow graves further up the beach, and after a time their bones were taken up and scattered, but a member of the immediate family took an arm bone or a shin bone (a radius or a tibia) and carried it for luck until it became uninteresting or a nuisance, when it was thrown away.

But a bone of a priest was never taken.

Each successive priest in his day watched on the sand-dunes.

Then came a day just like that day on which the great spirit man appeared. The sun came up out of the sea in a white sky as before and the sparkling spots danced and spread on the water and the waves were weary.

A priest stood on the sand-dunes. Away out on the ocean the great white thing appeared. It rolled with the water.

The priest ran to the slumbering people and soon the sand-dunes were lined with men and women and children who watched the unknown thing out on the sea.

The tide went out. They fully expected it to turn and come in, and to see Allambee with it. The story of him was as fresh in the knowledge of the tribe as if the happening of his going was one of only the day before. The priests, one after the other, kept the story green.

There not much work done that day. And all the conversation was about Allambee and the expected coming. The white thing was the first of many that came, and it was seen that white men came from them and sometimes white women were with the men.

These men and women were of the race that Allambee went to be the ancestor of, and to this race belong all men who go out black and return white.

WHY THE WARATAH IS FIRM

The whole George's River tribe were camped on the flat between the bouldered cliffs that stand up high on each side of the stream. The weather had been very dry. Hot winds brought the yellow dust from the and regions of South and Central Australia and they wilted the vegetation of New South Wales and parched the people. One of those droughts, so well known to us, was withering the land. Though the happening took place many thousands of years ago, and though the story may have been altered in the telling by so many fathers right down the line, the story of the drought is the same as that we can tell of such a dry time.

The river had not been in flood for many moons, or, perhaps, years. Fish and eels were scarce. Only the big holes had them. Those holes are very deep, especially in that part of the river that has great flat rocks lying athwart it and stretching out on each side of the bed. Seventy feet is considered to be the depth at many places.

Most of the people were lolling in the shade. Only the hardiest stood motionless on the rock bottom with poised spear, while the hidden baiters gently scattered fine pith from the cabbage palm or chewed up seeds of the macrozamia, to attract the fish and bring them to the surface. Warmeela, the son of the King, was the hardiest of all, and Krubi, his lubra, was never done warning him about the risks he took in war and in the hunting. Even now she stood under the myrtles, and with a waratah that she held in her hand she beckoned Warmeela to come to her.

Warmeela took no notice. Instead, he glanced to the west, for away over there great thunderclouds swelled slowly but surely up, and the faint zephyr that swung softly down the ravine ceased altogether. The hot air stood still. The only movement was the thrust spear as with a zip it pierced the water, and the quick kick of the impaled fish as he was suddenly lifted out and dropped into a crevice that prolonged his life for a little while, but in the water of which he soon struggled his last.

Then came the roll of thunder. The clouds blotted out the sun. A shade like the blackened haze of an eclipse spread over the river. One of the baiters went back to the myrtle scrub. Warmeela remained. Then the other went, and only Warmeela still stood by the hole. The tribe was moving back to a huge cave they knew of that had been formed by the rolling together some time long since, of several boulders. There was shelter for every man, woman, and child.

Warmeela's spear was poised. Like the cracks of millions of whips at the one time the first crash came and with it a frightful jagged fork of lightning. Warmeela was struck. His spear was hurled from his hand over the water, and stuck quivering many feet deep in a soft place on the opposite bank. There was a charred mark down its whole length, and the bone point was wrenched off. Warmeela lay prone amongst his struggling fish. A brother rushed to him and bore him back to the tribe.

Rain poured down. Roll after roll, crash after crash; thunder and lightning shook the hills. The wind came tearing through the giant gums and swirling amongst the shrubs.

Warmeela was unconscious of it all. He knew nothing of the consternation of his tribe. His old mother chafed his hands and the king gazed stupidly. Krubi, his pretty wife, held his head on her arm.

The storm rolled off again as quickly as it came, and then Warmeela opened his eyes. They were now useless. A print of a gumtree lay across his face, and the limbs were marked over his eyes. His sight was gone. A white streak appeared in his jet-black hair and one arm hung paralysed at his side. The next morning he tried to walk, and it was seen that he had a terrible limp.

Blind!

Now Warmeela was most fond of the honey of the waratah. The great *Doryanthes excelsa* produced much honey, but ants and gnats got that. Seldom did any aborigine regale himself with the juice of that flower, because he did not like the taste of ants nor the stings of flies. The waratah was different. Its honey, though less, is sweeter, and mostly there were no insects in the flower at all. But though it may seem strange to us, the bloom of the waratah was at that time very soft.

That was the statement of a broken-hearted native, whom the white called Griffiths, to the pioneer out Taralga way about sixty years ago. His real name was Coomerkudgkala.

Poor Warmeela. He had been so strong, so agile, so big hearted and so high-spirited. He now stumbled amidst the rocks. He would suffer none but Krubi to lead him. And often Krubi had to engage herself with those things that women did, but always before she was half through the task, Warmeela called her. If she did not come at once he went off by himself.

The waratahs were blooming again, for a year had gone by, and Warmeela often put out his hand hoping to feel one.

He still hated to be handed anything. He wanted to feel and fetch and carry for himself.

Two flowers bothered him. The big yellow *Podolepis acuminata* and the flower of the native Musk (*Olearia argophylla*) often deceived him, and once some other flower poisoned him.

One day Krubi, his beautiful wife, came upon him when his heart was sad and he was ill and depressed. She asked plaintively the reason for his sadness. Warmeela felt for her hand and answered slowly, saying that he did not know one flower from another. He said he would drink of the honey of the waratah, but he could not find it. He too often mistook others for it.

Krubi promised that she would find a way so that Warmeela should always know the flower he wanted so much.

She led him to the place where the lightning had struck. She found a mark of it on the rock and she followed it knowing not why. Warmeela was willing to hold her hand and be led. The mark lay straight on over the flat rocks and the boulders, to the eroded bank. It showed on the bare root of a gumtree that it had split. Krubi looked up at the shape of the tree and she saw that it was the one printed on her husband's face. She sat beside the gum and there she was inspired. She spoke, and Warmeela did not understand the words. No one knows what she said. After a time she got up, and bidding Warmeela to wait, she sped over the rocks and logs until she found the beautiful red waratah. She returned with it and held it close to the crack in the gumtree. The soft pistils were drawn up and they stiffened. Krubi held the flower to Warmeela, and when he felt the difference he clasped his big hand over it. He clasped too hard. He bent the red pistils. In that moment a big red light lit the sky. A red ball descended, lighting up the firmament in such a way as to startle all who saw it. Some screamed and rushed about.

Not so Krubi nor Warmeela. They knew what no one else knew. The prayer of Krubi had been answered and thenceforth Warmeela would have no difficulty in distinguishing the flower he loved.

THE FIRST CRAYFISH

Perhaps no white man, hunter, or fisher, was so clever at catching any sort of game as the blacks, and perhaps no "native race," not even the red men of America, about whom we have read so much, who were so painstaking in their snaring, their stalking, their lying in ambush, so shrewd and stolid and picturesque, showed the patience, the cleverness, the agility, the keenness that were the universal attributes of our blackmen. Clever writers about the Reds of the West have told how they rode, and how they ambushed, and of their relentlessness, but not one story shows that they had the bushcraft the equal of that of the Australian aborigine.

This story deals with the catching of fish. No lines, no hooks-just rush nets and bare hands, and spearing, and the spearing was only done when the fish was big.

Of all the fishers of the Shoalhaven people none was so clever as a certain Krubi. She left it to other women to dig the yams. She caught fish.

The camp was a permanent one. Its location was somewhere near the site of the bridge of Nowra. High rocks sheltered it from the southerly winds, and a deep forest prevented the westerlies from reaching it.

Krubi caught fish with her hands. She used a bait of meat (too bad, by the way, for us to have handled), and this she hung between her own shapely black feet. When the fish were ravenously fighting for the food, Krubi simply drew her feet up and up. But this "simply" is just the requisite thing, and therein do we white people fail. True it is, though, that our superior knowledge and inventiveness have given to us means whereby we can catch as the blacks did not; though the very ease with which we may get big hauls is the undoing of our catching, for we caught to waste. Blacks never caught more than filled their immediate need.

Slowly but surely Krubi drew the bait. The movement was so uniform that not a tremor disturbed the meat, and not a ripple appeared on the water. Then Krubi's supple arm straightened. The hand entered the water wonderfully cleanly, and it was gently lowered with the long black fingers closed on a fish. There was no escape for it. Quick as a flash it was drawn up and the dexterous toss that landed it was the acme of cleverness.

The men of the tribe made bark boats. They carved a great ellipse of bark from the turpentines and from certain gums, and wrenched it free without a crack. Yet never did they ring a tree, for they knew that the bush of Australia was their living.

We are cutting our living out.

The blacks caught the ends of the piece of bark - two men to each end - and rapidly see-sawed it over a smoking fire. The best smoke was that made by throwing the branches of the *Callitris calcarata* on the fire. When the piece had been smoked sufficiently they placed a heavy log in the centre, the smooth side of the sheet being uppermost, and bent it to form the sides and the gunwale. Then the ends were easily drawn together and sewn with rawhide or sinews of the kangaroo. The tiny crack was caulked with rushes and mud, and as a last means of making the ends watertight they were smeared over with beeswax. Tingles and thwarts bound with rawhide were fixed, and the whole craft was constructed in less than three hours.

Krubi stood by one day watching the boat-builders, and as she had become noted for her success at fishing she was allowed to show her interest in the work. Immediately the boat was launched she sprang lightly into it.

The other women of the tribe were aghast; never did they dare to enter a boat uninvited. But the men seemed pleased to allow Krubi to take advantage of the admiration so plainly bestowed upon her, and together they set off down the river in great glee.

Somewhere near its mouth there was a deep hole, and there the yabbies were unusually big. When this place was reached and the boat was beached the men set to work to fashion a net. Krubi remained in the craft and tried for yabbies. She had the usual piece of putrid meat, and breaking a part off she tied it to the end of a long stick. This she put into the water close to the big stones, and when it was bristling with clinging yabbies she drew them, clinging to the bait, right out and into the boat.

Catching yabbies was easy work. But in one haul there came up one bigger than all the rest. Amongst yabbies he was a giant. Krubi faltered when she picked him up, and a little spine on its head pricked her finger. The warm blood flowed upon the wet fish and it spread all over him.

This warm blood was a new and startling thing. Yabbies are not accustomed to anything as warm as human blood, and this one, startled as he was and being so big, jumped high in the air and landed with a splash back in the river. With great kicks he drove himself through the water, every now and then giving himself a mighty shake in an endeavour to throw off the warm liquid that was strange to him. On and on he went, down to the sea. The black men heard the splash and asked Krubi what had caused it.

Krubi excitedly told the story and showed her wounded finger.

Shortly after the net was set the people decided to pull further - to pull and sail on the current of the river right into the sea should the weather remain calm and the sea smooth.

They went round the point and into a sheltered cove, and there they hove to. Krubi was gazing over the side, when what did she espy but the big yabbie!

However, in a moment it had disappeared. She told about it, and many were the expectant glances and long looks that were sent overboard, but it did not again come into sight.

Many times afterwards fishermen of her tribe rowed round the spot, but it was not for some years that anyone again saw the curiosity. Krubi had grown middle-aged and had given up the pranks that she indulged in when she was young.

One day a son of hers caught a red yabbie. It was with intense delight that he hastened to the camp to show his mother the wonder.

She spat her disgust. It was not nearly big enough. It was red certainly, but it was far too small to be the one that had pricked her finger those long years ago. She said that there must he others and that this one came from them. She saw that a race of red yabbies, big and strong, was brought into being, and she knew that the first had been reddened with her warm blood.

THE CLINGING KOALA

There was but little of the habits of the indigenous fauna and avifauna of Australia that the aborigines did not well understand.

How many white people gave our native animals credit for the possession of the same senses and emotions as the human race has?

The blacks had a legend, or ascribed a reason, for all the little ways and tricks of birds and animals. Some of them, too, are very ingenious; some of them pure superstition.

Of the native bear they spoke little. Its humanlike cry awed them. It was "tabu."

They say that at one time the native bear and the fabled bunyip were close friends. Indeed, some averred that the bear is of the bunyip family. It always had the power of becoming invisible.

To prove this they tell of a black who essayed to catch a native bear that had its home in the fork of a big gum-tree somewhere near where the bridge spans the Wollondilly. In spite of the appeals and protestations of his people, he took his waddy and climbed the tree. He reached the bear, and just as he was about to club it the tree opened. The centre was rotted away, and into the hollow the man fell. His cries could be plainly heard outside, but no one dared to do anything to effect a rescue. He was left to slowly weaken and to go out in death.

Though this tale was told many times by the blacks, of course no white man credited it until somewhere in the seventies, when the tree was blown down. Then the bones of the aborigine were found in the trunk. There was no opening from the outside at the bottom of the tree. The bones were of great age.

The story says that the bunyip lived in the Wollondilly and a koala that lived near was on the best of terms with him. The koala's home was on the top of a mountain, and the bunyip made almost nightly excursions from the river at the foot, to sit with the koala and talk of ancient times. Many an aborigine had been almost seared to death by meeting the prowling bunyip.

When it was discovered that the horrible thing always travelled by the one path and frequented the top of the mountain no black would dare to be in the vicinity at night, and no one ever went to the mountain top. It was found that the meetings took place in the very early hours of the mornings, and it was thought for a long time that the bunyip did not leave his hiding place in the day time at all.

No other bear agreed with the friendship that existed between one of their race and a bunyip. The bunyip was hated, but the bears were loved for their gentleness, and their cry, plaintive as it is, reached hearts, and all koalas were safe. The flesh was never eaten.

Now bears argued that should the people find out about the strange friendship their security from molestation would be endangered. And they saw no chance of escape, for they could not travel fast enough. They remonstrated, but the erring bear took no notice. She heeded no warnings. She left her young one unattended while she philandered and meandered with the bunyip.

Then the bears took counsel. They had noticed the mystic markings on the sorcerer of the black men. They had-many of them-often watched the result of this peculiar painting with the clays. In watching they nearly closed their eyes. They pretended to be asleep, for they had seen that many blacks were not allowed to see the rites. The men allowed them to stay because they were "tabu."

All watchful animals, plainly wide awake, such as dingoes, native cats, the larger marsupials, snakes, etc., were all driven off; but the little koalas sitting in a fork, dozing, dozing, were supposed to see nothing.

And they were "tabu."

Yet all the time they were watching and they knew all about it. Therefore the bunyip's companion knew. Nearly all knew. One that was much larger than any other undertook to paint himself and get aid from the spirit that came to the call of the paint and the markings, and when the bear again went up the mountain leaving her young one unprotected the spirit that saw waited for her return. He caused the little one to spring upon the mother's back and to cling there night and day, so that the mother was not free to come and go and to fraternise with the bunyip as before.

The young one clung too tightly; it could not be shaken off.

The mother tried the pipeclay. She only brought the punishment to all the rest of her tribe. Therefore all young bears cling to their mother's back and she is so hampered that she never moves far from the spot where she was born.

And if you look closely into the face of a koala you may see the partially-closed eyes, and the peculiar parting of the hair on its face to correspond with the clay marks.

A BIRD LEGEND

The aborigines sometimes kept birds and animals as pets, but in all instances that may be enquired into it is found that the pet by some mischance or peculiar trait or impulse strayed into a camp and stayed there. However, this had nothing to do with the belief in an "affinity." Nor yet the belief in and recognition of a "totem." That possibly originated in a knowledge of evolution-in the settled idea that during the ages everything has changed in form-and no outstanding fact of Nature escaped being considered the beginning or the dwelling-place of an ancestor or an originator.

But something of a parody of this fundamental belief is the acceptance of an affinity in the shape of a bird or an animal that knows of its being related to a human and who acts as a protector of those of whom it is a family part. In this way the last full-blooded woman of the Cammaray people believed in the snake. She says that the black snake always indicates to her whether or not an undertaking of hers is to be successful, when a calamity is about to happen or has just happened in her immediate family, when she is personally threatened with great loss and whether or not the time be propitious for the doing of any important thing.

She tells many weird tales of warnings shown to her by her affinity. The lyre-bird, she tells, was the affinity of a man of her people away back in the time before history, and he had one as a pet. He was very proud of the fact that his bird mimicked so marvellously, and he arranged a competition. People who belonged to such birds as parrots, black cockatoos, wattle birds - those with a clear, distinctive call - assembled, and they listened to the lyre-bird not only imitating, but excelling each in its own song.

One bird was not claimed by anybody, and it sat disconsolately on a limb, apparently taking no notice of the proceedings; and then, just before dark, it made its effort.

The lyre-bird, noting low, imitated it perfectly. But the other bird was not finished. In another key it performed again, and still in another, until the lyre-bird was bewildered. It failed to follow; therefore we may now hear the great bird mimic as we stand, say, at Echo Point in the Blue Mountains, or under the hills of the Snowy or the Cann, going through all its repertoire, imitating not only every other bird, but every sound it has ever heard. But when it comes to the laugh of one it fails. The bird it cannot properly mock is the kookaburra. The lyre-bird man of the story was discredited, and therefore in later years such men were never of much account in the eyes of their compatriots, while those of the kookaburra, though it is recognised as an affinity of a much later date, are always people of great importance.

And by some strange coincidence we have taken the kookaburra to our hearts, and we picture him much more as the bird-representative of Australia than the emu which figures as such officially.

TWO WARATAH LEGENDS

There are many legends concerning the waratah - Australia's most glorious flower and all her own, for it does not occur in any other part of the world, while its supposed rival, the wattle, is as common in all parts of the Southern Hemisphere as it is in Australia. The aborigines wove some very pretty and fanciful stories about their prettiest bloom. Most of them come from the Burragorang Valley, though at least one must have filtered through from very far west, for in this story lies enclosed the fact that the waratah did in early tertiary times flourish in West Australia.

This story is one of the making of the waratah red. It was supposed, it seems, that it was at first a white flower, though that idea does not pervade the other stories of it. Still it was loved then just as much as it is now, and its whiteness did not detract from its charm. The day was away back in the alcheringa and it had been very still and very hot, and the whole tribe, with the exception of one man, lay amongst the bracken in the shade of big eucalypti and lesser myrtles and other scrub. The sweet-scented Sassafras grew there, too, and that other perfumed shrub, the *Olearia* or Musk, and without a doubt, the exquisite *Ceratopetalum* or Christmas Bush, as well. The spot was at the foot of very high bouldered cliffs that bounded a deep, clear-pooled river, and the one man who was not prostrated was fishing. All this was in a valley, and out from it the land was a parched and barren tract. The sun blazed down and the heat dazzled, and the sandy and gravelled ground was too hot to walk upon. Now not a zephyr moved the air. The season must have been spring, for the waratah blooms only in that season, always waiting until the cold of winter had retreated to the Pole to which it belongs, or to the regions above the clouds.

Most of the people were asleep. They had retired to the shade. They knew that great cumulus clouds would at length appear from beyond the west and that most surely they would bring thunder and lightning and rain and coolness. An infant - a very pretty child not yet able to walk and perhaps not yet entirely black, for aboriginal babies were born brown, and the black of them showed first under their fingernails and spread from there - crawled away from its dozing mother or whatever woman had charge of it, and the dogs were too indolent in the heat to notice it laboriously getting closer and closer to a tangle of *Hibbertia*, or Guinea-flower vine, through which stood the Waratah plant resplendent with gleaming white flowers. In there, coiled but alert, lay something else that gleamed - a watching black snake.

Now, the child was of the black snake totem, and, that being so, the reptile was its guardian, not its enemy.

As some of our children have done, the little baby put out its hand to play with the usually deadly thing, and just at that moment the guardian awoke. She missed the child at once. One hurried glance around and she saw the situation. There was the baby about to play with a venomous snake. Forgetting that the child was of that totem and that it would do her no harm, she grabbed a nullah and flung it with all her might, and the back of the snake was broken, and its blood streamed out. The only movement it was then capable of was a swaying of the forward part, and this part it placed around the baby.

Another missile was thrown, and, had the snake not been where it was, the child would certainly have received the blow and been hurt. The snake was again hit, as it, being the protector of the child, intended that it should. Slowly and painfully it unwound itself. The now frightened baby rolled away. The snake laid its injured self amongst the stalks of the waratah bush, and slowly its blood was absorbed as it trickled from the wounds. In a few days streaks of red were to be seen in the flowers, and by degrees the whole of them were so coloured, and therefore we have the bright and beautiful blooms of far greater quantity than the white ones.

It is certainly strange that the white waratahs appear to be much older than the usual crimson ones.

The last full-blooded woman of the Cammaray tribe says that she is a black snake woman and that the black snake is her guardian.

When a baby, her life was saved in a manner somewhat similar to the way the baby of this story was saved and it always warns her of approaching danger, and when her intentions, if carried out, will not be to her advantage. So sure is she of that, that she takes careful notice in summer, and she only undertakes serious matters in that season so that she may be warned by her black snake.

MIST AND A FRINGE FLOWER

It is said that many departed aborigines return to this earth in human form. A legend has already been written in which is the thought that blackfellows often slipped during their journey along the Milky Way through Magellan's Clouds, and came back here. Dense mists were supposed to envelop these returning people, for they were too considerate to make themselves visible suddenly and thus frighten their relatives. They remembered how frightened they themselves had been always when any not-understood phenomenon took place, and they took care not to willingly cause such consternation now that they were from the other world. Yet by inadvertence this was often done.

Aborigines were generally much frightened when mists came, and they often crouched in the shelter of crevasse or camp until they had cleared away. They feared the unseen, and they could not conjecture what fearsome thing might be hidden. They watched the curling, eddying vapour, and their imaginative and often artistic minds saw many fleeting shapes. There is a story of fire coming with a mist which is called "pouraller," and burnt stones near Appin were pointed out as a place where this particular mist often covered the country. No doubt the fact that volcanoes emitted fire with steam is responsible for this idea which has become somewhat distorted in its passage down the ages since Canobolas in New South Wales and Mount Fairy in Victoria and Mounts Gambier and Schanck in South Australia threw out their molten masses.

The strip of country between the Appin Creek and George's River was the home of a very powerful group. To-day the watershed drained by the Cataract and the Loddon rivers is one source of Sydney's Water Supply. The head of George's River is in the same locality, but it falls the opposite way and its waters do not flow into the Cataract Dam. On it are King's Falls; on the Loddon the Loddon Falls; on the other creek the Appin Falls. All are most picturesque, though the Appin Falls are now quite governed by the floodgates of the Dam. The real owners of this country roamed over the luxuriant forest. In our time the village of Sherbrooke was built there and Frank Knight's sawmill is responsible for the destruction of the beautiful woods. The natives travelled the peaty patch known to us as Madden's Plains in the days of their mastery, and from the edge of the Illawarra Range they saw the sight that we recognise as the most beautiful in the whole world. When they roamed towards the setting sun they went as far as the Nepean, which winds itself along the foot of the hills of the Blue Mountains.

Madden's Plains is the country of many mists. It was somewhere there that a pretty purple flower grew, and it was there that an old man died - an old man of story and of truth.

Before his burial his womenfolk sat in a little circle and manifested their grief. A son passed by in jaunty fashion just as if he did not care, and the old women ceased their lamentations and commenced upbraiding him in loud, angry, querulous voices. He answered them back, and it seemed as if a quarrel, bitter and vociferous, must ensue. Two other young men took sides with their comrade, and the whole camp would have been involved had not the undertakers come to bear away the body to its resting-place.

The spirit had gone. The Milky Way seemed to be closer than usual, and in the morning the whole county was enveloped in a thick mist. It swung up from the jungle at the foot of the range and swept by over the plains and the creeks and the scrub, and must have been lost in the clouds that surely hovered on the crests of the Blue Mountains.

No one stirred from the camp. But the women had not spent their desire to scold the man whom they knew was too callous to feel the death of his father. And he, of all the people, ventured forth into the mist. He had had enough of the tongues of the old mourners.

He had plucked a little stalk that bore several of the pretty violet flowers, and for want of something better to do, or in order to soothe his ruffled feelings, he sat beside a log and quietly and deftly tore the edge of the petals, making them nicely fringed.

Slowly the mist rolled away, and in its billowings was to be seen the form of a man. A short distance off he appeared again, only to be once more swallowed up in another wave. By this time the sorrowing women saw him and in frightened whispers they told the people. Then break after break occurred in the driven mist, and gradually the sun came through it. A short time after it had gathered itself together and had gone away, and the country was clear and crisp and damp, and the sunlight was warm. And slowly approaching from up the creek that we call Muddy Creek was a man. He had the form and the voice of the one for whom the women were grieving. His hands he carried behind his back.

Without a word he strode slowly to the young man, who still sat tearing the violet flowers. Of all the people he was the only one who was blind to the visitor. It was not given to him to see a spirit-man, just as it is not possible for white people to see what can be seen by the natives. Suddenly the hands came from behind the back and a nullah was swung down upon the head of the youth. Because the flower had three petals the spirit-man struck that many blows. There were three marks on the youth's head. The flower fell to the ground, and because it was damp and warm the seeds soon germinated and the resultant flowers had fringed petals. It is a lily. We know it as *Thysanotus* or Fringed Violet. Perhaps it is a pity it was ever called a violet. It is said by the blacks that it only opens in a mist, and that before the mist clears away the spirit of the slain youth has to tear every petal and make them fringed. The three blows are perpetuated in the wale or bruise-like mark on every petal. It is strange, surely, that so gruesome a story should have been told about such a delicate and beautiful flower.

There is a rather pretty story about the fringed gum-blossom, and in it is a reference to a sea and an island in the centre of Australia.

MULGANI

This is a true tale about some black people who lived in this country before any white people set foot in it - long before.

Unlike the other stories which are legends that have actually been told as legends, this was not told regarding one specific happening nor one particularised person nor persons. It was done by many. It may be called a type story. Just what is said the people thought was really thought by many, and just what is said the imagined people did was really done by many.

In that way it is brought before readers what was thought and what was done, though Mulgani is created to bring it all.

Read first what a tribe was. It was a very large number of people who were broken up into many groups, big and little. These groups thought themselves a family, and the names they had were family names. We whites call just a father and mother and their children a family. The aborigines considered that all children belonged as much to all the uncles and aunts and cousins as to the actual father and mother, and uncles and aunts were those men and women whose brothers and sisters the actual father and mother might have married, seeing that they belonged to the proper totems. So their idea of family was much wider than ours.

Mulgani was a pretty little aboriginal baby. She was born hundreds and hundreds of years ago.

Let me now tell you how to speak of the black people. You should say "aborigine" when you mean a person, but "aboriginal" when you mean the kind of person. For the bigger people who read this book I will tell that the word "aborigine" is a noun and the word "aboriginal" is an adjective. Therefore we say that a story (for instance) is an aboriginal story and the first teller of it was an aborigine.

Mulgani was a Katungal. Her people lived away down on the South Coast of New South Wales, at Twofold Bay. An atlas here would be a useful book to have beside you as you read, for in it you can see the names of the places.

Now there was to be a great ceremony at a pretty spot near where is now the Excelsior Coal Mine at Thirroul.

Mulgani's father heard about it. A messenger had arrived at Twofold Bay and he brought with him a piece of stick about a foot long and about an inch in diameter. It was a piece of waratah stem and on it were cut some marks. Some of these marks were just circles cut right round it, and between the circles little cuts were made that looked like four-legged stools. Then again there were spots or dots. The marks were a strange written language, for they could be deciphered by a few men of the people wherever the stick was shown. To be a messenger was no easy task, for before he could have his intentions understood, and before he could reach the readers of whatever tribe or group he wished to visit, he ran the risk of being misunderstood and perhaps speared. Of course he carried weapons with him. But when he came in sight of a camp he waited quietly, generally sitting on a log or on the ground. Then when he was seen he threw his spears to the ground. After being received he was allowed to go back and recover the spears. No one of the visited people were ever known to steal such spears. It is known, though, that messengers have been killed by mistake or mischance or for some serious reason and their weapons remained where they were laid down, and were found there long years afterwards.

Mulgani was only a few weeks old. She was not yet even black. She was a dark brown colour, but the real black that commenced under her fingernails was spreading, and soon she would be as black as any aborigine could be.

Her father and mother were watching her very closely, for they were anxious, not wishing her to be too long becoming as black as they were. She had been, as was usual, kept covered with fat - the fat of the wombat if such animals were native to the district - and powdered charcoal. Her aunts saw to that, and it was done for two reasons: first that she might appear black, and secondly that she might be put out in the sun and burnt by it without it hurting her tender skin. The wind, too, would have chapped her, but the covering prevented it.

Now her father was very fond of flowers. He had made many trips to the mountains that lie away to the west of Twofold Bay - the Muniong Range we call them - and he had seen all the trees and shrubs and plants of the bush. He had picked some and had brought them back to Mulgani's mother before Mulgani was born, and the mother wished that she could go to the mountains and get some for herself.

And now this messenger had come with the message-stick to tell the Karungals about the big ceremony, and although Mulgani was only a few days old, the father and mother intended to go to it.

But the father had to attend a night school for a few nights.

He had not ever been taught how to prepare *Styphelia* berries or Geebungs (called *Persoonia* by the botanists) and *Astrolomas* or Ground berries. These berries were often eaten raw, but because Mulgani's father had been told that he must not eat them unless they were cooked he had never eaten them at all. He got quite enough of other foods that were not forbidden him. Of course they were mostly cooked too. Now that he was with many others going on a very long journey, taking his wife and little child, it was considered that there might be some difficulty in obtaining enough food, therefore no article must be neglected, and there were certain ways for all the people to live, and those ways were taught them at the proper corroborees. If they were not treated correctly there was the danger of magic being in them. Of course we can see that the magic was only the poison that so many fruits have, and which is nullified by some sort of preparation. This idea of magic was not of a lot of primitive people with no sense nor reason at all. The people were primitive, but they had sense and knowledge, and there is a basis for every thought and every custom. No doubt some time away back in the ages a blackfellow was made sick by eating the green geebung, and that happening was ascribed simply to magic. We must not belittle a blackfellow because he speaks of magic. Why, see this: - Only a little while ago I heard a woman-a white woman-say that waratahs should not be kept in a house because they brought bad luck. What is that but blackfellow's magic.

And for no reason at all. No one ever became unlucky, no one ever died, or was made sick, by the waratah. There is no basis for the idea. Then that white woman was far more ignorant than the blacks in that respect. That some flowers do make us sick is well known. If we do not call the reason magic, then it is because we have found out that it is the superabundance of pollen that is the cause of the sickness. The wattle flower is one of those in which there is danger because of its great quantity of pollen.

Anyhow tiny Mulgani's father was very anxious to go to the school, and he was very pleased when he found that the king had ordered such a school to be held. Everybody of the group that lived around Twofold Bay could attend.

Many schools were secret, and only the teachers and the special scholars and those who had already been to such schools were allowed to be present. Such schools were those at which things were taught and ceremonies were enacted that might be described as sacred. And all schools were termed by white people "corroborees," and for a long time they were thought to be nothing more than dances. There were dances, too, and they also are called corroborees.

After the school those who were to travel to the great ceremony set out.

The way was long and in places difficult. Mulgani was often carried by one or other of her aunts.

Sometimes the party was right on the beach, sometimes on the sandhills and sometimes in the scrub. But never did they go too far from the sight and the sound of the waves. On the sand-hills there were very pretty flowers - the *Mesembryanthemum*, a very brilliant and dainty vine and just at the bases the big yellow *Hibbertia*, and gleaming purple masses of *Hardenbergia*.

The Malelucas were in blossom and the sweet scent that they give out was a great pleasure to the travellers, though of course Mulgani was far too young to notice such a thing as that.

They came to the Shoalhaven River. The party travelled up it on the high rocky sides for many miles. Then they came across a camp of people of their own tribe, but of course a different group. Here they were welcomed and given the best of food. It was better than any they had got since starting out.

While they rested in this camp Mulgani's father went out and gathered the *Styphelia* berries and the *Astrolomas*, and what he did not cook he put in the dilly bag that was carried by his wife. It was delightful to see how the wallabies were cooked and how the best parts were given to those who should by right of birth or age have them.

The travellers stayed there for about a week, and during that time every day Mulgani was put on the ground out in the sun. She was quite happy, and her father and mother showed with pride that she was now all black.

Many of the people of this group joined the travellers. They had heard of the intended ceremony and the summons and were awaiting the coming of this party.

Soon they came to the country of the tall, swaying cabbage-palms and the staghorns and the treeferns. Many of the big detached rocks had the *dendrobiums* with their long creamy fronds of flowers, and the sweet scent was better by far than that of the tea-trees they had passed through, for the flower of the *Dendrobium speciosum* is more sweetly scented than almost any other in our Australian bush. There is, however, one other that must be mentioned here, though the travellers did not see it. It is the *Symphyonema paludosum*. It grows only in swampy places, and such swamps do not occur anywhere along the route taken, though they are not very far away for they are on the top of the range under which the ceremony took place.

In another week the party reached the spot and they found a big gathering of people. Some had come from over the range.

There were fires and smoke and feasting and singing and the beating of drums. There were corroborees, some of them, such as dances, for the whole of the gathering; and there were also those secret ones for only the special people.

Mulgani was a toddler before she was brought back to her own country.

THE BLACK SATIN

On the South Coast of New South Wales (not the Illawarra coast, which is not the South Coast) is a wonderful tract of deeply undulated forest, wild and jungled bush. The highlands of this big territory overhang a strip of well-scrubbed and verdant bush which rolls north and south, showing the creeks and gullies by the deepness of the purple, and which, eastward, thins out to paddocks of perpetual grass with broad waters spread in them, and they in turn slip downward to curved edges and curved broad beaches of gleaming yellow sand broken into scallops by lion-like promontories that gaze out - ever out - over the great blue expanse of Pacific Sea.

These highlands are but foothills, though far-flung, of Australia's Great Dividing Range. They have been pressed to where they are by great weight. It is as though one day they will be pressed on and will cover the jungle and will be engulfed out over the beaches.

The jungle is the home of giant gums and dense myrtle, of umbrageous fig and tall palm, of sassafras and supplejack. The millions of shafted trees rear their topmost boughs up into the clouds and stand as great pillars, and the voice of animal and bird reverberates as the human voice does amongst fluted pillars of a great cathedral. But the movement of wallaby and bandicoot and bushrat, of the lyre-bird as he scratches, of the spotted native eat and the wallaroo, is silent, for there is a carpet of fallen leaves that allows no more sound than does the Axminster or the Brussels of the mansion.

All the wonder growth of our best Australian bush in this piece of country. Gullies are deep and dark. Rolling ridges are rounded and ferned. Down in the depths the creeks lie still. All the ferns, all the mosses, all the deep-green, rank-grown underscrub hem the chill waters of the little sunless creeks and close them about. Trailing vines and heavy myrtles make the gullies almost impenetrable. Up the slope of the mountain the scrub is less, and massed burrawangs hang out their fronds as if to repel the wanderer.

In one of the densest of the gullies, where the *Eugenias* and the *Ceratopetalums* hide the carpet of fallen leaves, lived a family of satin birds. The King of the Family was jet-black.

Down on the shores of the great wide Casuarina-fringed lagoons lived a family of aborigines. Their king was jet-black, and his totem was the satin bird of like colour. When the hunters tired of fishing, and when they wearied of crossing the sand-dunes and the glaring, shimmering beach glaring and shimmering on every fine day of summer- to poke off the mussels and spear the butterfish and groper, they pushed through the *Ceratopetalums* and the burrawangs, and, following the tortuous bed of the principal creek amid the ferns and the moss and the vines and the myrtles, gradually ascending, they entered the sub-tropical patch where the ferns were huge and lank and staghorns clustered on rocks and trees, and the beautiful *Dendrobium* clung, and the supplejacks and leatherwoods and bangalow palms ran up in slender height, and that pretty massive parasite - the wild fig - made its umbrageous shade, as has been written. Here they rested.

No shaft of sunlight ever penetrated through this dense foliage. Never did the fallen nor clinging plants here feel drying wind or see a sunbeam. It was never dry.

The porcupine pushed his spikey body through, slowly raising and lowering his banded quills, and the fat bandicoot snouted for roots, and sleek tiger-cats lay in wait for the pretty green tree-snake, and for other venomous reptiles; the brown-banded and carpet and diamond snakes twined among the vines or lay coiled between the damply warm roots.

Above, in the upper branches, the colonies of pretty flock and top-knot pigeons clattered, and a little lower the parrots and gill-birds shrieked. Below them the wrens and tits mingled with fantails' both black and brown, and down on the ground the little seed-eaters darted, while the coy lyre-bird stood and made his mocking calls or scratched powerfully to unearth his meats-the grubs and bugs and roaches of the damp underscrub.

When they had rested enough the straying hunters, with singleness of thought, arose and pushed on and up.

A wall of rock rose sheer with just one narrow cleft down which the water rushed or fell, and on the level crest of that a view above the figs and other tops out over the *Ceratopetalums* and burrawangs, and across the shimmering surface of the lake above the now hazy sand-dunes and beach to the wide, flat, blue sea, met the admiring gaze of the men.

But there was still far to go.

A wide slope down again to the level at the back of the ridge where the water of the creek was a miniature lake with just the narrow cleft cut through the wall, and down where the vines grew again and the eucalypti were mingled with turpentine.

A few hours' tramping and struggling with impending vines here, and they came to the gully of the satin birds. The darting, timid birds with the shining greenish plumage sat stock still while they watched the party of hunters. The jet-black king had chosen a burnt patch on the side of a *Richea*, and there he clung, his colour and that of the grass-tree making him almost invisible.

Then one of the hunters spied the home of his favourite grub on the side of this grass-tree, and as he detoured to get it the black satin thought he was discovered and he sprang out. He was very fat and heavy, and the surrounding scrub was thick, so he flapped awkwardly into the entanglement of *Clematis* and *Eugenias*.

This was his mistake and proved his undoing. Like a flash the nullah was flung, and with a grunt of satisfaction the aborigine rushed forward and seized his victim.

Now one of the party was the brother of the king of the group, and he, too, was of the satin bird totem. He asked to be allowed to examine the king of the satin birds, and, without touching it, having satisfied himself that it was really the totem of his father and himself, he said that it must not be again produced so that he could see it. The man who killed it must hide it, and it must be cooked and eaten quite out of sight of any man whose totem it was.

The black bird was hidden in the bag that was worn attached to the rope of fur around the black man's waist.

The giant range was still far ahead and there were many miles of this wooded country to be traversed before the party could reach the blue top that met the sky, and they pushed on until it was too dark to go further. No food was eaten that evening, and the dead satin bird remained fully feathered in the bag of the captor.

During the night he rolled in his sleep and the bag was emptied.

The black satin slipped beside the bird man.

In the morning when he awoke he saw what had happened, and because he was a bird man he was very frightened. He had been taught that he must never handle the king of the satin birds. The whole family was to him tabu, but the most tabu was the black one.

People who were tree people or flower people, or indeed of any other totem, could handle the satin bird and eat it.

However, as the custom was, he said nothing. All day he wondered what would be the ill that would come to him.

Once, in going over the deep creek by traversing one of the hundred logs that lay from bank to bank - a creek that wound along the foot of the enormous range - he slipped, and a jagged broken limb caused a deep wound in his leg and he thought that that was perhaps the punishment.

After that the real ascent, with all its difficulties and dangers, began. The men were behind a high pointed mass of mountain rocks that held a huge stone poised on its top and they were shut in by that and the surrounding steeps and by a wall of thousands of feet which was yet to be climbed, and then the sun went out.

Unnoticed, the day had changed.

Buried as they were in the dense forest the sky was out of their ken.

It had dulled. Deep clouds had spread over it, and now as they scaled into a higher air they found it to be raw and chill and a wind was blowing with a grim, steady persistence that foreshadowed rain in plenty.

Presently a fierce gust swept along the side, and after that the heavy rain fell. The black men huddled together and were at first undecided about what to do.

Presently it was agreed that the best thing was to return to the shelter of the gully behind the sharp-topped mount, there to await the passing of the rain. They lit fires and the man with the black satin turned his back to the rest to pluck it, and he took fire from the little heap, and out of the sight of the others he cooked his bird.

The son of the king ran no risks. He, too, parted from the group, and did his own cooking and he ate in silence. They all had berries and pieces of wallaby flesh. Only the satin was to any of them a totem thing.

Suddenly there came a roar from the mountain side. Huge boulders were crashing down the steep. A rock had given way, and it came on, bringing others, and felling trees, and the group of blacks were right in its path. They scrambled up and each ran, holding the cooked food in the hands, to escape.

The falling mass was almost upon them. It was coming far more swiftly than any of them could run. Though it was impeded by trees so also were they by the scrub. The wound in the leg of the king's son prevented him from going as fast as the others, and the man with the piece of satin bird in his hand stayed to aid him. He grasped the arm of the other and they sped on, stumbling and falling, but progressing. Then their hands slipped together and each touched the totem.

Then they were paralysed. They fell. A big tree crashed. The rest escaped. They got out of the path of the avalanche of rocks.

When the falling debris was stilled and the rain was ceasing and the wind was lessening they retraced their strides and they found the unlucky pair.

This put an end to their adventure. All knew what was their own totem, of course, and all knew that an outraged ancestor would have a revenge when he saw a disrespect, whether intentional or not. The ancestors were all jealous gods and they found ways of visiting such a sin upon everyone connected with it.

They returned the way they went out. There were the usual lamentations and the usual mourning period. The wives especially were required to show great sorrow, and by painting themselves with white clay, and pulling out their hair, and by cutting themselves in various places, particularly straight down the middle of the head so that blood ran over the face and down the neck, they satisfied the onlookers that they were genuinely grieved. No one ever went exactly to the place of the tragedy. Therefore, when, long years afterwards, white men were clambering about that steep of the great Curockbilly Range, they found the bones, and a derelict remnant of that once virile family told enough for me to write the true story of the black satin.

www.ingramcontent.com/pod-product-compliance
Lightning Source LLC
Chambersburg PA
CBHW031223090426

42740CB00007B/682